GREAT —— BRITAIN

Explore the best coastal walks, castles, road trips, city jaunts
and surprising spots across England, Scotland and Wales

Yaya Onalaja-Aliu & Lloyd Griffiths

Hardie Grant

TRAVEL

Contents

Introduction iv
About the Authors vi

Introduction

As you have probably already gleaned, we're Yaya and Lloyd, and we both love to travel.

Over the years, we've travelled a lot. And we've found that even the smallest bit of information can absolutely transform a trip. It's why we love to share what we've learnt, what we love and what we wouldn't care to repeat if we came back (case in point – going horse riding in a snowstorm in Iceland. The scenery we passed was probably beautiful, but we couldn't see a thing so have no idea! We spent all our energy trying to stay on our horses and power-blink all the snow away from our eyes.).

By sharing our travels, we've connected with a community of like-minded voyagers who've helped us along the way, too. Shout-out to everyone who sends us recommendations on social media – you're the real MVPs.

Which brings us to this book: a guide to some of the best places to explore in Great Britain.

Like many Brits, we were guilty of considering holidays at home as not being 'proper' travelling. It's not that Britain isn't special or beautiful; it's just that we took it for granted. It's so easy to start exploring your own back garden, so it felt like if we hadn't gone through the discombobulation of airport security, we somehow hadn't earned our 'travelling stripes'.

Ironically, the thing that changed all that was jetting off to European locales like Paris, Brussels or Amsterdam when we lived in Edinburgh. We were obsessed with seeing all the sights – the architecture, the history, the people – but after returning home from a trip to Brussels, it dawned on us how so much of what we were travelling

Our first trip together was back in 2009 when we ventured over to Amsterdam, full of excitement and curiosity – and a distinct sense of cluelessness, too. Our naivety fuelled our adventure and led to some (retrospectively hilarious) misadventures: eating awful food at sky-high prices, missing out on interesting sights and poor timing. Seven months later, a bit of research and experience under our belts, we returned to Amsterdam. And what a difference it made! We spent less money, got to truly sink our teeth into the city and did even more amazing stuff than we could have fathomed on the first trip. It made us properly fall in love with the city and truly taught us how important it is to have the right information when you're planning a trip.

After several years of travelling together, and over 100,000 photos later, we finally decided to write about our adventures on our blog – Hand Luggage Only. Our online abode was named for our love of luggage-lite adventures, although we definitely don't shy away from more plentiful packing when the destination demands it.

So much of what we were travelling for was right on our doorstep

for was right on our doorstep. From medieval cathedrals and incredible castles to white sandy beaches dotted with palm trees, ski resorts with views to rival the Alps and vineyards that wouldn't look out of place in the South of France – we've got all of that right here in Britain.

And then 2020 happened. Covid-19 threw a big spanner in the works when it came to travelling the globe to seek out adventure. Like many people, we found ourselves making a big deal out of small trips – hopping in the car or on a train to visit somewhere a few hours' away. And boy have we found some unexpected treasures in this green and pleasant land.

Whether you're a fellow local, brand new to Blighty or a wide-eyed wanderer looking for adventure, we want to inspire your next Great British escapade and give you the information you need to make the most of it. There's no point just telling you how delicious a slice of cake is – we want you to be able to devour the cake yourself (not before you've taken that perfect Instagram photo, of course). Mmm, cake!

Speaking of 'Great Britain', for those not already in the know, we thought we'd clarify where exactly we're talking about. Great Britain is the largest of the British Isles (the island made up of England, Scotland and Wales). We'll also be using it to refer to smaller islands that belong to these three countries. By contrast, the United Kingdom stands for the sovereign nation, the United Kingdom of Great Britain and Northern Ireland, sometimes confusingly referred to as Britain.

For the sake of this book, the broad strokes difference between Great Britain and the UK is that the latter includes Northern Ireland and the former does not. That means you won't find any Northern Irish places in these pages (our recommendations for which could fill a whole other book!). It's also a wonderful place to explore, especially the coastline!

There you have it! That's who we are, what we do and, hopefully, a quick insight into what this book is all about. We've condensed our knowledge based on exploring Great Britain over many years, as well as our time living in England, Scotland and Wales, to bring you the very best this eclectic isle has to offer. So, what are you waiting for? Get those bags packed, grab your camera and stock up on snacks for your impending adventure around Great Britain. 🖐

About the Authors

I'm **Yaya**, and here are a few facts about me. I grew up in Nigeria. I love to dance. I hate uphill climbing but appreciate the view at the top. I love to eat – my favourite food is plantain (always fried). I get really invested in trash TV, and I'm a repository of garbage celebrity information (yes, I'm that person who pauses the TV to tell you what other movies the whole cast have been in). I can't sing at all, but I don't let that stop me belting out a tune in public. I also tend to make up the lyrics (most of which make no sense when I stop to think about what I'm singing).

I'm **Lloyd**, and I'm the one who loves to plan our adventures (I'm also the designated map reader). I've been fortunate to travel since I was a wee child. Through my parents' love for sharing new places with me, I found a passion for exploring near and far. I love a hearty bowl of poutine, would do anything for a Sunday roast and will drink any other Brit under the table when it comes to tea.

Hand Luggage Only started when we met at university. We'd both save all our extra dosh to book trips away (we still went to all our lectures, promise!). We soon set up a blog to record our awesome memories, travel challenges and love for perfect pubs, secret city spots, countryside escapes and delicious puddings. Since graduating, we've continued to explore. From hiking the ancient trails of Peru to searching for rhinos in Nepal, we've had our fair share of wild experiences. But some of our greatest adventures have been right here in Great Britain: an island that we adore and are proud to call home.

We love connecting with our followers and hearing all about their adventures too! Come say hi at **handluggageonly.co.uk**

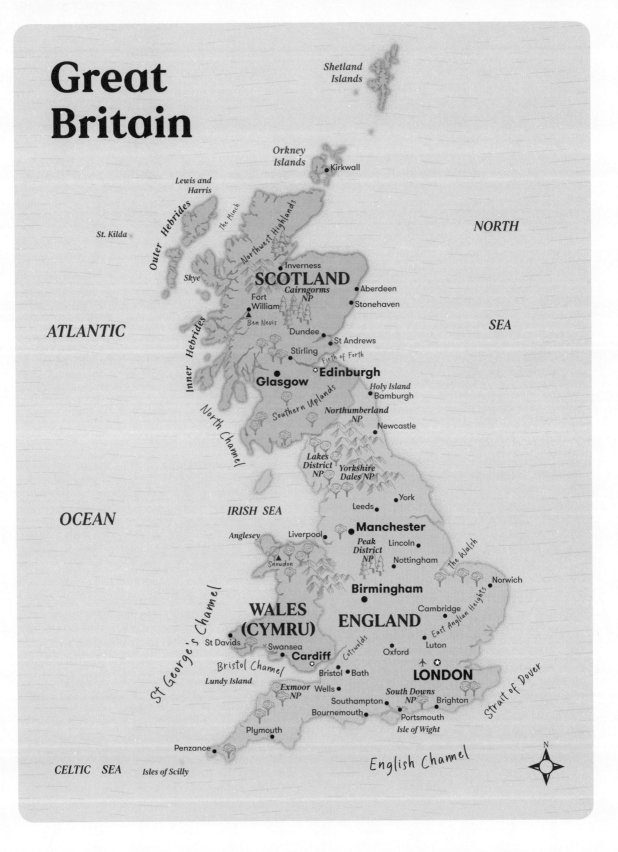

Great Britain

Coasts, Peaks and Paths

Mind-blowing hikes
to get you moving

From meandering trails to mountain treks ... Great Britain has it all

↑ Views after views after views on the hike to Hallin Fell in the Lake District

Our island nation is a special place to explore by foot. There are thousands of miles of trails and walkways, suited for any and all abilities, criss-crossing our charming countryside. From gruelling treks that test your endurance to easy-breezy strolls perfect for an afternoon mosey, we've selected the best of the bunch.

And if you're strapped for cash, you needn't worry. Hiking can be one of the most affordable activities – whether you're a budget or bougie traveller. Plus, it's an environmentally sound way to explore our beautiful island and take in some incredible views.

Just remember, as with all hikes, you should listen to local advice (tourist information centres are a great place to start) as there can be seasonal changes to routes. This might not be the Australian outback or the Rocky Mountains, but some trails can be dangerous if you're not experienced or if you venture out in bad conditions.

When you're hiking, always follow the marked trails and route maps. Lots of areas around Great Britain have designated zones to protect vital ecosystems. Also, be sure to tell someone where you're going, your intended route and when to expect you back. We might sound like your mother, but it's essential that you keep people in the loop when on a hike, especially the more remote trails that can take weeks to complete.

We almost forgot the food! Prepare accordingly with provisions and plenty of high-energy snacks and water. A hike with no treats just isn't a hike, in our opinion. Can someone pass the Jammie Dodgers? ✍

Summit of Snowdon

⚲ WALES

As the highest mountain in all of England and Wales, Snowdon is incredible for a challenging day hike. There are six different hiking routes to get to the summit, but it's worth noting some are much tougher than others. One of the easiest is the Llanberis Path, which is just shy of 10 miles (16 kilometres) long. This means you can get up (and back down) in one day. Just be sure to depart earlier in the morning as it typically takes around 6–7 hours to complete. It's a rocky climb, so wear ankle-supporting hiking boots. Eagle-eyed hikers might spot fossils in the rocks near the summit. It's thought these are from when the mountain region was underneath the seabed hundreds of millions of years ago.

A scenic shortcut
Take the mountain railway to the top and hike down from the summit itself. This way you'll have much more time to enjoy the incredible vistas with a lot less effort.

⬆ Sunny days on Abereiddy Beach

Pembrokeshire Coast Path

♀ WALES

Stretching almost 200 miles (321 kilometres) along the beautiful Welsh coastline, the Pembrokeshire Coast Path is one heck of a trail to dip into and enjoy. Taking in towering cliffs, ancient volcanic headlands and a heap of charming beaches, it's totally awe-inspiring.

Similarly to the South West Coast Path (*see* p. 10 ☞), this would likely take you around two weeks to complete (depending on how big your steps are). But we tend to tackle bite-sized sections now and again, which makes the trail much more manageable.

If you're starting on the south-east section, ramble around the tiny coves and bays near Tenby before heading further west towards the Green Bridge of Wales (Pont Werdd Cymru in Welsh) – a colossal limestone archway (*see* p. 102 ☞). Then in the north, near Cardigan, check out Cwm yr Eglwys, a centuries-old church ruin that's falling into the sea. It's said these buildings are part of the ancient kingdom of Cantre'r Gwaelod, which, according to legend, was swallowed up by the water many moons ago.

Mountaineers rejoice
If you walk the entire route of the Pembrokeshire Coast Path, you'll end up scaling over 35,000 feet (over 10,600 metres) of ups and downs. That's higher than Mt Everest! Which, incidentally, was named after George Everest. No one knows his exact place of birth, but his family estate was in Wales, specifically Powys.

Northumberland Coast Path

📍 **ENGLAND**

Stretching 62 miles (100 kilometres) in length, the Northumberland Coast Path is one of the best British hiking routes for history buffs. Along the route from Cresswell in the south to Berwick-upon-Tweed in the north, you'll see historic remnants from the last 7,000 years dotted all across this coastline. We recommend setting aside a week to complete the trail or dipping in and out at your leisure to enjoy the sections that intrigue you most.

As you ramble along the unspoilt coastline, be sure to stop off at the totally pristine Bamburgh Beach where, just shy of the shore, you'll spot Bamburgh Castle. From here you're just a short walk at low tide to Holy Island (*see p. 48* ☞).

Sea food, eat food
Hankering for a bite to eat? Pop into the historic fishing village of Craster with its picturesque harbour and country pubs, which offer some amazing local seafood. It's like heading back to the 1800s, but with much better fish and chips.

Fife Coastal Path

📍 SCOTLAND

At 116 miles (187 kilometres), the Fife Coastal Path is pretty sizeable and will take a week or so to complete fully. Starting around Newburgh, it follows the North Sea coastline to Kinkardine. It's a stunning hiking route and a great way to explore Fife, a vast peninsular with stone-cottage fishing villages, towns and rugged coastlines.

Along the way, you can choose to walk the smaller additional trails around Tentsmuir Forest before heading beyond the historic town of St Andrews to Anstruther. Work up an appetite from all that sea air, and then fill up on some tasty fish and chips right on the harbourfront. Eat in or dine al fresco while spotting seals that frequent the shore.

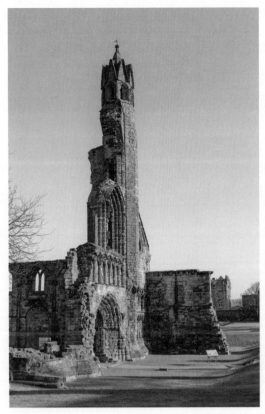

↑ The incredible ruins of St Andrews Cathedral

The missing link
One additional section of the Fife Coastal Path is the Elie Chain Walk (between Earlsferry Beach and Shell Bay). It's Fife's very own *via ferrata* (iron path) and is pretty epic if you're looking for a challenge. You'll need a few hours to complete it, sturdy shoes and an adventurer's spirit. Never attempt this at high tide or during blustery conditions, and watch out for local warnings.

Diabaig Coastal Circuit
📍 SCOTLAND

Although a bit of a grind, the Diabaig Coastal Circuit is worth the trek if you're looking for a little bit of a challenge. Starting at Lower Diabaig, walk away from the coast towards Loch Diabaigas Àirde, which is right next to Upper Diabaig. The whole route is 7.5 miles (12 kilometres) and will take 4–5 hours to complete.

As you continue, head further east towards Bealach na Gaoithe viewpoint. It's the perfect spot to chill out with some incredible vistas. Finally, take the extremely challenging route west beyond Alligin Shuas and back towards Lower Diabaig. This section can be difficult as you climb in height and battle overgrown vegetation. We're not trying to put you off, but this one's really for the more experienced hiker. Even so, it's worth every aching calf and sore thigh for the views.

↑ Stopping to take in the view of Loch Diabaigas Àirde up in the mountains

Get spirited away
While walking, keep your eyes peeled for Kelpies – legendary Celtic water spirits that dwell within Scotland's lochs and have reportedly been sighted in the area. Folklore states that they take the shape of horses but also have human-like features. We were totally eagle-eyed, but, alas, none appeared!

Vistas and vantage points in England's oldest national park

Monsal Trail

📍 ENGLAND

Around 8.5 miles (14 kilometres) long, the Peak District's Monsal Trail is perched in the very heart of England's oldest national park. Starting in Bakewell and finishing around Chee Dale, the trail itself is well paved and easier to visit for those with accessibility needs.

Weaving through the picturesque dales, the trail follows a historic railway line. The trains are long gone from this route, but you can still meander through the historic tunnels and over the iconic Monsal Head Viaduct. Before heading out, grab some of the world-famous Bakewell tarts from one of the town's many bakeries. You'll be glad you did when you're hankering for a sweet treat along the way.

Cotswold Way

◉ ENGLAND

We have a big soft spot for the Cotswolds! It's one of those picture-perfect areas of Great Britain that's so beautiful to explore. Think chocolate-box houses, rolling hills and centuries of history. If that's your thing, you'll totally love this area.

Better still, the Cotswold Way is a mighty trail that encompasses 101 miles (164 kilometres) of walkways and public rights of way (see p. 13 ☞) that go from the trailheads at Chipping Campden to the Roman city of Bath.

Along the route, you'll get to explore Broadway Tower at the top of Broadway Hill (one of the highest points in the Cotswolds), not to mention the ancient village of Broadway itself, where you can wander past quaint limestone cottages and stop off at a teahouse. Other great sights include Sudeley Castle, the ruins of Hailes Abbey and the Tyndale Monument.

↑ Yaya hopscotching in Broadway

Two Moors Way

⚲ ENGLAND

The Two Moors Way is another epic hiking route that spans 102 miles (164 kilometres) between the north and south Devonshire coasts. Starting in Ivybridge, or Wembury Bay (near Plymouth) for a slightly longer version, the route heads inland via Dartmoor National Park, passing Knowstone (where you can warm your cockles at the 13th-century Masons Arms) and through the heart of Exmoor National Park, before finishing in Lynmouth. Along the way, make sure to see the Tarr Steps, a medieval stone bridge overlooking the River Barle.

Both parks are great for spotting wildlife, especially Exmoor (see p. 153 ☞). If you're hiking between March and July, be sure to stick to the trails and tread carefully. There are lots of ground-nesting birds that call this moorland home and are sensitive to surprise guests!

The Monk and the Merchant Walk

⚲ ISLE OF WIGHT

Just shy of 5 miles (8 kilometres) in length, the Monk and Merchant Walk is a great hiking trail to complete while exploring the Isle of Wight. Starting on the island's south coast at Blackgang, you'll pass by the medieval oratory of St Catherine's before heading further inland along a loop towards the Hoy Monument (erected by a Russian merchant to commemorate Tsar Alexander I's visit to Great Britain in 1814) and back around to the shore. The route takes 2.5–3 hours and is perfect if you fancy a little dabble into hiking, without being committed to some Everest-like expedition! A word of warning: this route can get a bit blustery at times, so take a windbreaker with you.

↑ Sunset in Lynmouth

South West Coast Path

♀ ENGLAND

Being one of Great Britain's longest trails at over 600 miles (965 kilometres), it's unlikely that you're going to smash the whole route in one go. That being said, you can certainly give it your best shot, or do what we do: choose the sections that interest you most.

The trail stretches from Minehead on the Somerset coast all the way around to Poole in Dorset, taking in some of the best coastal views in the south of England. Along the way, be sure to check out the Valley of Rocks overlooking the Bristol Channel or visit the iconic Land's End, the most westerly point in England.

If you love a good mythic monument, stop off at Tintagel Castle, which, folklore says, was the birthplace of King Arthur himself. Or take some time to chill at Watergate Bay **(see p. 166 ☞)**. It's a surfer's paradise and an incredible place to relax after a long day on your feet.

⬆ The incredible Valley of Rocks

Hallin Fell Hike

♀ ENGLAND

Aside from the stunning vistas, one of the great things about hiking up Hallin Fell in the Lake District is that it's relatively easy – perfect for beginners or those who want a shorter hike with lovely views.

The hike is 1.5–2.5 miles (2.4–4 kilometres) long, depending on which trails you choose, and although you do climb in height, it's slow and gradual, so it won't take your breath away (well, the views across the lake might). The whole ramble will take a couple of hours.

The hike starts next to Howtown, which is easily reached by boarding a historic 'Steamer' boat from any of the stopping points on Ullswater **(see p. 176 ☞)**. From here, mosey your way up towards St Peter's stone church and head to the summit itself.

Celebrate with cake
After completing the hike, ramble on back down to Howtown to the little tearoom where you can pick up a pot of tea, tasty cakes and Scottish tablet. Yum! Remember to take some cash (card payments can be an issue).

South Downs Way

♀ ENGLAND

Another whopper of a hike, at around 99 miles (160 kilometres), the South Downs Way stretches from the coastline around Eastbourne (and Birling Gap) to Winchester. Although it's a toughie in terms of distance, the lack of steep climbs means it's achievable for most people with reasonable fitness levels.

Be sure to look out for the Long Man of Wilmington. This ancient monument of a figure holding two staves was once carved into the slopes of Windover Hill and discovered at least 400 years ago (the white chalk carving has since been replaced by painted concrete blocks, but it's still very impressive).

Plus, you'll get to take in the views across the Seven Sisters chalk cliffs and see the Bignor Roman Villa. Why not stop off in Amberley like we did and spend the night at Amberley Castle – how often can you say you've stayed under the same roof as Queen Elizabeth?

Acorns and arrows
National Trails are typically signposted with a small acorn icon. You can also follow public rights of way (routes that run over private land, but which the public has the right to use). These are marked with different-coloured arrows, depending on who's allowed to use them. Yellow routes are for walking only; blue means horses and bikes are allowed too; purple routes can be used by non-motored transport; and red routes are open to all traffic. Hop off the marked route to explore areas of interest along the way. Pub stop, anyone?

Pennine Way

♀ ENGLAND (AND A LITTLE IN SCOTLAND)

Known as the 'Backbone of England', the Pennine Way stretches a whopping 268 miles (431 kilometres) from Edale (see p. 168 ☞) all the way to the Scottish Borders. If you fancy following the whole route, spend a few days relaxing at key spots along the way, to rest, recuperate and give yourself plenty of time to savour the scenery. As the first National Trail in England, it takes in breathtaking sights like High Force (see p. 103 ☞), High Cup Nick glacial valley and Hadrian's Wall (see p. 161 ☞).

Respect, protect, enjoy
Always make sure you follow the Countryside Code, which lays out the responsibilities for hikers when accessing public rights of way. If you're unsure, most visitor centres will be able to advise on this. Alternatively, visit gov.uk and search 'Countryside Code' for more guidance.

Responsible Travel

Tips to keep your conscience cleaner

If you love to travel as much as we do, you're used to your conscience reminding you to be greener. Climate change is very real. From the food you eat to the transport you choose, it's never been so important to take stock and make conscious choices to reduce your carbon footprint.

Beyond environmental concerns, we all have a duty to be respectful when we're away from home. Choosing to travel domestically, rather than flying thousands of miles away for your next holiday, is a great start. You'll keep your carbon emissions down while supporting local businesses and environmental and archaeological projects right here at home.

With that in mind, here are some essential travel rules that we live by. Wherever you're headed, we hope they'll help you stay mindful of the impact you have.

1. Choose the train and not the plane

Although regional airports can take you the short distances between major British destinations, trains are a far eco-friendlier way to get around. Choose the train over flying from London to Edinburgh, for example, and you'll reduce your CO_2 emissions by around 84 per cent. And by the time you've travelled to the airport, cleared security and taxied the runway, you could be halfway to where you're going by rail.

Trains in Britain can be pricey, but there are ways to keep costs down. Book your tickets up to three months in advance online and always travel during 'off peak' times if you can. Plus, don't forget to buy a railcard (railcard.co.uk) if you're planning on making a few longer trips a year. Different options are available, depending on your circumstances, but they'll reduce your fares by a third.

2. Eat seasonally and locally

We all know strawberries don't grow in Britain in the winter. If you're eating an Eton Mess in January, it means they've either been flown over or intensively harvested in heated sheds. Imported food has a considerably larger carbon footprint than a seasonal, local alternative. Head to restaurants that offer seasonal menus and prioritise locally sourced ingredients, including meat-free options. They won't have been shipped by lorry from afar, and you'll also be supporting the local economy.

3. Volunteer trips

Be part of the solution by volunteering in the region you visit. Look online to find beach clean-ups like we did when we visited Newcastle. Lots of national parks, like the Lake District, have volunteer programmes. This is great if you're in the area for a longer period of time. Check in with local organisations before you travel so you can give something back while enjoying the region. And if you can't find an initiative, create your own. Set yourself a mantra to never leave a beach without litter picking. It'll quickly become a habit, and every little bit really does help!

4. Pack light and smart

If you do need to fly, pack light! We're not saying weigh every pair of socks and take just one pair of underwear for a whole trip – could you imagine?! But there is an environmentally sound reason to reconsider squeezing in that extra coat and fourth pair of shoes. The more you take on the flight, the more fuel is needed to get all that luggage off the ground.

5. Offset your carbon footprint

Even the savviest of eco-minded travellers has an impact. Carbon-offsetting is a way to redress the balance. Head to websites like woodlandtrust.org.uk where you can calculate your carbon footprint for various transport options or activities. Find a scheme where you can contribute to environmental projects that aim to negate your impact.

6. Choose responsible lodgings

Before you book accommodation, check out a place's 'green credentials'. As a consumer, your money talks, so head for hotels that look for ways to reduce their own footprint. For instance, Grays Court Hotel in York donates all its old newspapers to a local hedgehog sanctuary and composts all organic waste.

7. Plan your routes

Embrace a good plan! Trust us, planning goes a long way when it comes to being a more responsible traveller. Not only can you be more efficient in the transport routes you take but you won't be darting back and forth to visit spots when exploring a new region. Plus, having a firm driving route before you travel will save time, meaning there'll be more of it for having fun.

8. Take longer trips

While taking shorter trips throughout the year is so much fun, any kind of transport is going to have an impact. It's better to travel less and stay for longer – giving you the chance to really get to know a different region and see more of what's on offer while you're there. If you do want to go away more frequently, keep the shorter journeys for places closer to home.

9. Be better in the bathroom

Having freshly laundered bedding and fluffy towels every day is a luxury the planet can't afford. When you're staying in a hotel for a short amount of time, reuse your towels and bedding for the duration of your stay. Bring your own toiletries so you don't have to open those little bottles of body wash.

10. Respect the communities you visit

Be mindful of the impact that your presence might have on local places. For instance, if you're visiting a sacred site, be sure to check the rules around covering up so you don't cause offence. The same goes for archaeological and historical places of interest. Be considerate so you don't unintentionally cause irreparable damage. For instance, you might really want to take a photo of Magna Carta in Salisbury Cathedral (*see* p. 131 ☞) but the 'no photography' rule is there for a reason: to protect it for future generations.

Whenever you're not sure, ask. This way, you know that you're being respectful, polite and considerate of the communities and sites you interact with.

11. Go electric

Electric is one of the greenest ways to travel, and that goes for cars, too. Many rental car and car-sharing services now offer the option of booking an electric vehicle. We did this when we visited North Wales. We drove over 100 miles (160 kilometres) and didn't have to stop to charge up the whole time we were there.

12. Limit single-use plastic

Yeah, we all know about this one, but you'd be surprised how much more plastic can creep in when you're travelling. Forgo bottled water and ask for tap water wherever possible. We've lived all over Great Britain and have always drunk tap water. While the mineral content can be different, it's all perfectly drinkable. We think Welsh and Scottish water tastes the best, while southern England's water is a little harder. Always pack a reusable flask and coffee cup to fill up on the go.

From Royal to Ruin

Fascinating and
photo-worthy fortifications

↑ Eilean Donan Castle on Loch Duich

So much of what has shaped Great Britain happened behind the battlements of its incredible castles. The key decision-makers of the land used to live within these walls, establishing laws, rearranging religion and cementing cultural norms, the evolution of which is still embedded in British life today. Beyond what went on inside them, these historical relics are also proof of architectural prowess, engineering ingenuity and the vast wealth their owners enjoyed.

If you're looking to cash in on castle-mania, it might be worth signing up for a membership with English Heritage – a charity that manages more than 100 castles, forts and defences – for unlimited access to all their protected places, some of which are featured here. In Scotland, there's a similar offering from Historic Environment Scotland, and in Wales there's Cadw – the Welsh Government's historic environment service.

To say we're obsessed with British castles would be something of an understatement. It's just so awe-inspiring to roam the same halls as some of history's most fascinating figures and to marvel at buildings that have stood their ground for centuries. We're suckers for stories, too, and boy do these castles have a great back catalogue of intriguing tales to discover. So, in the tradition of all great castle-worthy stories, once upon a time ... ☞

Dunnottar Castle

📍 SCOTLAND

Dunnottar Castle in Stonehaven, on Scotland's north-eastern coast, looks like something out of a fairytale. Solitarily standing on a lonesome rock, jutting out into the sea, it's surrounded by dramatically jagged coastline, which you can ramble around at your leisure. Given its fantasy feel, it's not surprising to learn that the castle was once home to a lion. Yes, you read that right. While it's mostly a ruin, there are some rooms still standing, giving you a sense of the grandeur that once was.

Edinburgh Castle
📍 **SCOTLAND**

Sitting high above the city, Edinburgh Castle practically beckons you to visit. It looks like it's always been here – and that's not far from the truth. People lived on this site long before the castle as we know it existed, its perched position making it ideal for defensive lookouts.

The castle was one of the most besieged in Britain and has changed hands quite frequently. Nowadays it's an iconic landmark for the city and home to the Honours of Scotland: the oldest surviving set of Crown Jewels in Britain. Listen out for the One O'Clock Gun, which is fired every day at 1pm (you'll hear it across the city centre), except on Sundays, Good Friday and Christmas Day. It's a tradition that harks back to the late 1800s, when ships on the Firth of Forth used it to set their clocks.

Fantastic freebie
Fancy visiting the castle for free? Every year Historic Environment Scotland hosts Doors Open Days throughout September, where you can visit Edinburgh Castle and hundreds of other heritage buildings for free. Tickets tend to be limited, though, so be sure to book in advance.

Eilean Donan Castle

♀ SCOTLAND

Built by Alexander II of Scotland in the 13th century to protect this part of Scotland from Viking invasions, Eilean Donan Castle in the Scottish Highlands has a colourful history, but it's probably more famous these days for starring in a number of TV shows and movies, including *Highlander, The World is Not Enough* and *Elizabeth: The Golden Age*. Sat on its own island, connected to the mainland by a footbridge, and set in the Kintail National Scenic Area, it's worth a visit for the views alone. Eilean Donan makes an ideal stop-off on our 'Big One' road trip (*see* p. 208 ☞).

Fit for royalty and every budding explorer!

Glamis Castle

📍 <u>SCOTLAND</u>

Glamis Castle is the ancestral home of Queen Elizabeth II's maternal family line, and is where her grandmother lived and her younger sister, Princess Margaret, was born. Exhibits include a letter Queen Elizabeth wrote about the summer holidays she spent there and official invitations for the royal weddings. It gives an interesting insight into the royal family and explains why Scotland holds such a special place in the Queen's heart. It's been open to the public since 1950 but remains home to the Earl and Countess of Strathmore and Kinghorne.

Something wicked this way comes ...
Glamis is the name of the titular character's home in Shakespeare's *Macbeth*. Turns out Shakespeare was great friends with the earl who owned the castle at the time he was writing the play.

Stirling Castle

📍 <u>SCOTLAND</u>

A who's who of Scottish history have laid their heads at Stirling Castle, including Mary, Queen of Scots, who was crowned there, and James VI, who later became James I of England and Ireland. It's also where the oldest football in the world was discovered – there's even a record of Mary Queen of Scots playing a game, found in one of her diaries.

Over the years, the castle has had periods of being abandoned, but it's been restored to its former glory and is open all year to visitors, with the exception of Christmas Day and Boxing Day; there's also reduced hours on New Year's Day.

Lindisfarne Castle

◉ ENGLAND

Lindisfarne Castle sits on Northumberland's Holy Island (just half an hour's drive from Bamburgh). Several times a day it gets cut off from the mainland when the tide rolls in and the road to the island disappears beneath the water.

Once a defensive fortification between Scotland and England, the castle dates back to the 1500s, while the island's history stretches back much further. In 793 CE, Lindisfarne was attacked by the Vikings, marking the beginning of the Viking Age (see p. 48 ☞).

It's positioned perfectly on a mound with a rather steep, albeit relatively short, climb to get up to. There are a few shops on the island, too – be sure to pick up some of the famous mead (an alcoholic drink made from honey) – and the expansive priory ruins are also worth exploring.

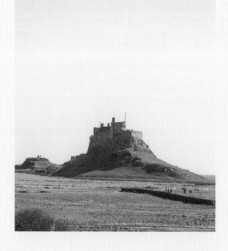

Time and tide wait for no man

Be sure to pay particular attention to the tide times (they will be signposted before you get on the road and also available online, so check on the day you plan on visiting), as it comes in very fast and you can get in trouble really quickly.

Bodiam Castle

♀ ENGLAND

East Sussex's Bodiam Castle dates back to the 1300s, when it was built by Sir Edward Dallingridge and his wife Elizabeth to protect the local area against the French during the Hundred Years' War. Nowadays there aren't any invading French folk, but the moat and castle structure remain as a rather well-preserved ruin.

Unlike some of the other castles on this list, Bodiam relied on a moat (rather than a high vantage point) to defend itself. That means it's much more accessible today, with no stairs to get inside from the carpark.

Bamburgh Castle

⚲ ENGLAND

Northumberland has no shortage of castles – it's home to more than any other county in England – but even with all that choice, Bamburgh stands out and absolutely has to be visited. For starters, it has a written history dating back to 420 CE, making it one of the country's oldest. In the years since, it's been ransacked by Vikings, been home to kings from Henry VI to James I, and was the first castle in the world to be destroyed by gunpowder in the War of the Roses. (Did you know author George R. R. Martin based his *Game of Thrones* book series on this ongoing struggle for the English crown?) Explore the staterooms, grand hall, grounds and beach beyond at your leisure.

A legendary history
Arthurian legend has it that Bamburgh is the site of Sir Lancelot's castle, Joyous Garde.

E-TRAITORS' GATE

Tower of London
⚲ ENGLAND

Known for its use throughout history as a prison – it's where Guy Fawkes was held captive after the failed gunpowder plot to blow up the Houses of Parliament – the Tower of London was also an opulent palace fit for the royals who lived there. It's a London icon and one of the country's most popular tourist attractions. This UNESCO World Heritage Site is home to the Crown Jewels, include the Sovereign's Sceptre with Cross, which contains the largest top quality cut diamond in the world.

Get keyed up
Don't miss the Ceremony of the Keys – a 700-year-old ritual that takes place in the evening when the tower is 'locked up' for the night. Tickets are free, but you need to book in advance.

Windsor Castle
⚲ ENGLAND

Let's be honest, Windsor Castle needs little introduction. Home to the royal family, it's easily one of the most iconic castles in England. Hop on a train from central London (about 30 minutes) and you'll arrive right at the gates of the castle itself. Just make sure to book your tickets before you go to avoid disappointment. Check in advance to find out if any special events are planned as certain areas might be closed depending on the day. And when you arrive, check to see if the Royal Standard flag is flying – if it is, it means the Queen's at home.

Windsor Castle is every bit as impressive as you might imagine. You'll find yourself in awe as you wander through its many stately rooms, taking in the lavish furniture and furnishings, impressive paintings and objets d'art. Plus, you can sneak a peek at the Queen's finest porcelain crockery.

Arundel Castle

⦿ ENGLAND

Established on Christmas Day, way back in 1067, Arundel is one of England's most iconic castles. It's the seat of the Duke of Norfolk – passed down through generations of the same family since Edward I.

While it's still a family home of epic proportions, you can explore some of the staterooms, bedrooms, the keep and the magnificent grounds. As it requires regular maintenance, the castle isn't open all year-round, so check the website before you visit.

Afterwards, you're only a short walk from Arundel Cathedral (a beautiful Gothic revival church) and a 15-minute drive from one of our top accommodation picks, Amberley Castle. And if all that grandeur has got you in the mood for some fine wine, then you're just 30 minutes away from Tinwood Vineyard (see p. 58 ☞).

Leeds Castle

♀ ENGLAND

Confusingly named, Leeds Castle isn't in Leeds at all –
it's much further south in Kent. A castle in some form has
been present on the site for 800 years, with the current
iteration opening to the public in 1976. It was the home
of no fewer than six medieval queens and a palace for
Henry VIII and his first wife, Catherine of Aragon. Henry
was responsible for transforming the castle from a bare
fortification into an opulent royal residence. Situated on
an island and surrounded by a moat, it's like something
lifted from the pages of a storybook. More recent additions,
including an aviary and a maze, make it a fun place to while
away an afternoon.

Beaumaris Castle
♀ WALES

Perched on the island of Anglesey, off the north-west coast of Wales, Beaumaris Castle is one of Wales's finest historic buildings. Built almost 800 years ago by English King Edward I, it was originally part of his plans to conquer North Wales, but because of a cashflow problem it ended up taking decades to get the thing built and it was never fully completed. What is there to see is no less than impressive (its designated as a UNESCO World Heritage Site). We were awestruck by the architecture and the sheer size – it's truly one of Wales's finest.

Caernarfon Castle

♀ WALES

Caernarfon Castle dates back to the 13th century. It's the grandest of Edward I's Iron Ring of Castles – built to control the native Welsh population – and where the investiture of the Prince of Wales took place in 1969 (that's when he officially received his title – a bit like a coronation). Architecturally, its distinct – the castle has an hourglass design (roughly in the shape of the number eight), which gives the castle two wards instead of just one.

You can see the King and Queen's Gates, walk around the upper and lower wards and check out the Black Tower, the Chamberlain's Tower and the Eagle Tower, arguably the most elaborate. All castled out? The town walls of Caernarfon are connected to the castle, so be sure to set aside some time to explore the local area.

Caerphilly Castle

♀ WALES

Known for the crumbly cheese that originated here, South Wales's Caerphilly is also home to a splendid concentric castle (where walls are built in concentric circles, providing an impressive line of defence) – the first built in Britain almost 800 years ago.

Then it was home to Gilbert de Clare, 7th Earl of Gloucester, who hoped it would help him maintain control of the historic county of Glamorgan. You'll notice the south-east tower has fallen foul of subsidence – it leans out over the water at an angle of 10 degrees (that's more of a lean than the Leaning Tower of Pisa). And make sure to pop into the Great Hall with its elaborate windows. You'll feel like you've stepped back in time.

Conwy Castle

📍 WALES

Another UNESCO World Heritage Site, Conwy Castle in North Wales was built in the 1200s by Edward I, further establishing his power in the region as part of his conquest to take over Wales. The rooms themselves might have gone, but the ruins are still impressive. Spend a few hours exploring the outer and inner wards, wander the grounds and walk the town walls, too. In Conwy, keep your eyes peeled for the smallest house in Great Britain.

A photo for the ages
Capture the perfect photo of this regal relic by heading across the road bridge (next to the castle). Alternatively, there's a little bank next to Benarth Road that has a great view, too.

Treasure Islands

Magical shores
to set sail to

↑ Cycling around Tresco in the subtropical Isles of Scilly

Islands always evoke a sense of adventure. Maybe it's classic childhood tales of pirates and buried treasure, a pining for *Robinson Crusoe* levels of isolation or the extra effort it takes to get to them – whatever the reason, there's no denying hopping on a boat for a taste of island life makes for an unforgettable trip, wherever you are in the world.

The British Isles, of which Great Britain is the largest, is home to some 6,000 islands, with around 136 that are permanently inhabited, so there are lots to choose from. From the Outer Hebrides to the Channel Islands, each has its own individual personality, offering travellers something unique. Whether you're an adrenaline junkie, a wildlife wanderer or just want to sit on the beach with a good book, there's an island here to suit.

We've picked our favourite isles to take you over the water to somewhere special, with no *Lord of the Flies* vibes in sight. Each entry includes some key travel tips to avoid any castaway conundrums, how to get there, and what to expect when you've made it. ⚓

The Skye's the limit when it comes to island gems across Great Britain!

Where the dinosaurs roamed
📍 ISLE OF SKYE

The Isle of Skye is a treasure trove of gorgeous natural sights. Look out for the Old Man of Storr – a huge rock up in the hills that's an iconic part of the islands – and the Fairy Glen, a beautiful turquoise waterfall. Throw in the fact that it's fairly easy to get to and you'll soon understand why it's such a popular destination for holidaymakers. It's also not short of incredible natural history. Skye is one of the few places in the world where dinosaur fossils from the Middle Jurassic epoch have been discovered – there are even fossilised dino footprints dotted around the island!

Don't forget: insect repellent – you'll need it to ward off the midges in summer.

How to get there: Skye is connected to Kyle of Lochalsh on the Scottish mainland by the Skye Bridge, so you can drive over. There are also three ferry ports on the island for a more scenic journey.

Prepare for people
Hotels and other accommodation are very limited, particularly in summer months, so be sure to book in advance. And if you are travelling in peak season, expect it to be busy in some spots as the infrastructure struggles to cope with the influx of traffic.

Subtropical sunshine
📍 THE ISLES OF SCILLY

The Isles of Scilly archipelago, off the coast of Cornwall, is home to the most southerly point in the United Kingdom. And thanks to the Gulf Stream (the warm ocean current that originates in the Gulf of Mexico), the islands are so warm that they're regarded as subtropical. There are over 140 islands, but the main ones are St Mary's, Tresco, Bryher, St Martin's and St Agnes.

St Mary's is probably where you'll arrive as it's the biggest; Tresco is one of the best to base yourself (it's where we stayed) – there are a good smattering of cottages and holiday homes to rent here; Bryher is delightfully rugged with some of the most dramatic scenery (look out for Hell Bay, the site of many a shipwreck on the islands); St Martin's is famous for its amazing beaches; and St Agnes is the smallest. At low tide, a beautiful sandy bank is revealed, connecting St Agnes to Gugh (see p. 120 ☞).

Don't forget: to carry some small change with you. They have honesty shops here (we saw quite a few on Bryher) – unmanned stores where you take what you want and leave the money you owe. You won't be able to get change for big notes or pay by card in shops like this.

How to get there: Fly from Cornwall to St Mary's – journey times vary between 20 and 60 minutes, depending on which airport you leave from – or catch a ferry from Penzance.

You might even spot some whales on the boat trip over!

Huffin and puffin

📍 **FARNE ISLANDS**

Just off the coast of Northumberland lies this archipelago of 28 islands, of which three are accessible to visitors. Often referred to as the 'Galapagos of the North', there's an abundance of wildlife here (whales, seals, dolphins and lots of sea birds), and it's easily one of the best places in England to spot puffins. Depending on when you visit, you'll probably get up close and personal with the thousands of non-human residents. Make sure you pack a pair of binoculars to look the part.

Don't forget: to make a back-up plan. Have some alternative ideas to explore the local area – like a visit to nearby Bamburgh Castle (*see p. 27* ☞) – in case the sea is too choppy to travel.

How to get there: Four private companies offer boat trips between April and October from Seahouses Harbour.

Un-loch the Outer Hebrides

📍 **ISLE OF LEWIS AND HARRIS**

Lewis and Harris (or Harris and Lewis, depending on who you're speaking to) is the main island in the Outer Hebrides, but people have always referred to them like they're two different places. It's easily one of the most beautiful spots in Scotland. There are lots of idyllic beaches with white sand and azure waters – a tropical paradise, albeit without the palm trees and baking heat.

Natural beauty aside, a visit is a prime opportunity to learn more about Scotland's rich history. Across the island you'll find stone circles, standing stones, Norse buildings and other fascinating ruins.

Don't forget: your wind breaker – the island's most northerly point, known as The Butt of Lewis, appeared in the Guinness World Records a few years back for being the windiest place in all of the UK.

How to get there: Take a ferry from the Isle of Skye or from Ullapool in Ross and Cromarty. You can also arrive by plane from Glasgow, Edinburgh or Inverness.

If it's good enough for the Vikings ...

♀ SKOMER AND SKOKHOLM ISLANDS

Once upon a time, these two Welsh isles were home to the Vikings, which is how they got their names. Both islands are also Sites of Special Scientific Interest with a fascinating history – there's evidence of human occupation dating back to the Iron Age. They're also renowned for birdwatching, and you can book a number of birdwatching tours from the mainland. Skomer is home to the largest colony of Atlantic puffins in southern Britain and half of the world's population of Manx shearwaters.

Don't forget: to pack a bag. You can stay overnight on Skomer and Skokholm, with the latter being a bit more off-grid as it's further out and takes a little longer to get to.

How to get there: Catch the boat from Lockley Lodge in Marloes.

Habitat hiatus
You can visit between April and September – except Mondays, when the wildlife gets a break from us humans.

For feathers and freedom

⚐ LUNDY ISLAND

Set in the Bristol Channel, Lundy makes a great daytrip, especially in the summer (though you can visit in winter, too). It's beautifully desolate – great if you want to get away from the hustle of city life. Its jagged cliffs and foggy weather have caused many a shipwreck near its shores. But it's not all bleak – this is a haven for nature lovers, not least of all because of its puffin colony (see p. 192 ☞). Keep an eye out for dolphin pods on the ferry ride to the island.

Don't forget: your toothbrush. It is possible to stay overnight on Lundy. There are 23 self-catering properties to pick from, including a 13th-century castle, a late Georgian gentleman's villa and a converted lighthouse, all managed by the Landmark Trust.

How to get there: From March to October, catch the ferry from Bideford or Ilfracombe – the crossing takes about 2 hours. From November to March, you can arrive by helicopter in just minutes.

A northern star

⚲ SHETLAND ISLANDS

This collection of around 100 beautiful islands is tucked high up in the North Atlantic – the most northerly places you can go to in the British Isles. There's a strong Scandinavian influence because they use to be owned by Norway and only became part of Scotland around 500 years ago. You'll find hints of this heritage dotted all around the islands.

We visited for Up Helly Aa – a dramatic Norse fire festival held in January to mark the end of Yule. If you can make it for that, it's well worth braving winter temperatures. If not, there's so much more on offer all year-round – with Norse settlements to visit, local delicacies to savour, boat trips to explore 'secret coves' and birdwatching. We recommend picking at least two islands to visit, including Mainland, which is the largest.

Don't forget: to keep your eyes peeled – you might be able to spot the Northern Lights.

How to get there: Board the ferry from Aberdeen or Kirkwall – it's a slow-going 12–13-hour journey, so settle into your cabin, kick back and relax. You can also arrive by plane from Aberdeen, Glasgow, Edinburgh, Kirkwall, Manchester or Inverness. Book island-hopping cruises once you arrive to pack in as much as possible.

Mutton dressed as mutton

When visiting Shetland, don't forget to try the traditional dish Reestit mutton. It's mutton (a sheep that's older than 18 months) that's been brined and dried to preserve it. It's traditionally enjoyed in a soup or pie, but you can also eat it cold.

Sacred sweets and scenery

📍 **CALDEY ISLAND**

There's evidence of early Britons living on Caldey, just off the Pembrokeshire shoreline, for over 10,000 years. It has been home to the Cistercian Order of monks since 1929, but monastic life has existed here, on and off, since the 6th century. Nowadays, the monks still undertake their divine duties, but the island is open to visitors, too.

Catch a boat from Tenby – once you've disembarked, explore the trails, see the Old Priory and visit the historic monastery. Make sure you try the chocolate and fudge made by the monks themselves. Visit their chocolate 'factory' (a large sweet-smelling kitchen) and buy a few treats to take home (if they can make it that far – ours didn't!).

Don't forget: Sundays are a no-go. That's when the island is used exclusively by the monks.

How to get there: Take a 20-minute passenger boat ride from Tenby (from Easter to the end of October, weather permitting).

Where seals outnumber people

📍 **RAMSEY ISLAND**

With its population of only two people, Ramsey Island is not the place to come for buzzing crowds. Saying that, you will find plenty of company. In mid-August, the island becomes a haven for Atlantic grey seals who come ashore to breed. Owned and run by the RSPB (Royal Society for the Protection of Birds), it's home to countless seabird colonies and peregrine falcons that nest on the island.

Don't forget: to visit in spring or summer – the island is only open to visitors between 1 April and 31 October. You'll need to pay an entrance fee (unless you're an RSPB member) on top of your boat ticket.

How to get there: Catch a boat from the St Davids Lifeboat Station in St Justinian with tickets from Thousand Island Expeditions in nearby St Davids.

A holy-moley habitat

📍 **HOLY ISLAND OF LINDISFARNE**

The tidal island of Lindisfarne is perched just off the coast of Northumberland. In the 8th century it was raided by the Vikings – its importance as a Christian centre meant this raid in particular marks the start of the Viking Age in Europe.

Nowadays, you can explore the ruins of the priory, pop into the 500-year-old Lindisfarne Castle (see p. 25 ☞) and stop in the independent shops selling crafts, coffee and souvenirs.

Don't forget: to check the tide times before heading across. Each day, the sea cuts off the island, flooding the road. This sounds pretty cool until you realise you can be swept away!

How to get there: Drive along the roadway that connects the island to the mainland.

Irresistible isolation

♀ ST KILDA

Located around 40 miles (64 kilometres) off the north-west coast of Scotland, the St Kilda archipelago marks the final frontier of the Outer Hebrides. This makes it a pretty special place to visit and one of the best in the Scottish Islands for nature-lovers. It's home to the highest sea cliffs in the UK and, as such, it's an important island for sea birds. Come here for the most unspoilt Atlantic landscapes in Scotland, a medieval village and dramatic cliffs and rock formations at every turn.

Don't forget: St Kilda is pretty remote. We recommend booking a daytrip from the Isle of Skye (or organise to camp on the island) with Go to St Kilda. Bring plenty of snacks and water with you. The journey will take around four hours each way, and the ocean can get very choppy.

How to get there: Book a boat trip with a charter operator (some are only available during the spring and summer), either from the Western Isles, Skye or mainland Scotland.

World-class wildlife
St Kilda was one of the first locations in Scotland to be designated as a UNESCO World Heritage Site for its natural beauty.

Home of the world's rarest apples

♀ BARDSEY ISLAND

Just shy of the Llyn Peninsula, Bardsey is known as the island of 20,000 saints for the number of holy people thought to be buried there. Plus, depending on who you ask, the final resting place of Merlin himself (and even King Arthur). Over the centuries, it's been home to a huge monastery – ruins of the 13th-century Augustinian St Mary's Abbey are still standing. Just being here will feel like you've journeyed back in time.

It's also home to the Bardsey apple. The only remaining tree of this variety was discovered on the island in 1998, making its apples the rarest in the world. Nowadays, you can buy a descendant of this very tree to grow your own Bardsey apples at home.

Don't forget: to charge your phone! While you can just come for a daytrip, you might prefer to stay in one of the island's traditional cottages. Just don't expect luxury (or electricity) here – the accommodation is pretty basic.

How to get there: Passenger boats operate from Porth Meudwy between March and October, weather permitting. You'll be able to spend three or four hours on the island before making the trip back.

Walk in the footsteps of giants

📍 ST MICHAEL'S MOUNT

No visit to Cornwall is complete without seeing St Michael's Mount, a tidal island you can walk right over to (via the centuries-old causeway) at low tide. Legend has it, it was once home to Cormoran, a giant who lived within the caves and had a penchant for gobbling up the local children. Yikes! Thankfully, Cormoran was slayed by Jack the Giant Killer and won't be bothering you on your visit, so you can explore the medieval castle, its gardens and the pretty village and harbour in peace.

Don't forget: to get up early. If it's a clear morning, head to Marazion Beach for one of the best sunrises over St Michael's Mount.

How to get there: By foot from Marazion in Cornwall, a short drive from Penzance.

Explore an ancient kingdom

♀ ISLE OF WIGHT

One of the biggest islands in the UK, the Isle of Wight is steeped in history, beautiful coastlines and chocolate-box villages. Once an ancient island kingdom called Wihtwara, it's home to thousands of years of human history and is the richest place in the UK for dinosaur fossils. Our favourite tourist spots include towering chalk stacks the Needles (*see* p. 102 ☞); the olde-worlde village of Godshill that's been around since before the Domesday Book; and St Catherine's Oratory – a medieval lighthouse and epic spot for views across the island (*see* p. 9 ☞).

Don't forget: to bring your wellies. Pair your trip with some tunes by visiting for the popular Isle of Wight Festival. It's a vibrant, sometimes muddy, four-day event with something to suit most music tastes.

How to get there: Arrive by car ferry via Portsmouth, Southampton or Lymington. Alternatively, you can travel as a foot passenger from Southampton, Portsmouth or Southsea (the latter takes just 10 minutes).

An ancient kingdom filled to the brim with history, tunes and royal homes

A Welsh beauty with heaps of history

📍 ANGLESEY

A few miles from Snowdonia National Park (**see p. 152** ☞), Anglesey is Wales's largest island (and the name of the principal area it's in). It's seen a lot over the years – a takeover by Irish pirates, the Romans before them, Vikings, English and even becoming the most southerly place in the Norwegian Empire. That means there are historic spots aplenty, like the medieval Beaumaris Castle (**see p. 32** ☞) and Din Lligwy, the ancient Roman village ruins.

There's lots of natural beauty to explore, too. Island-hop over to Ynys Lawd – a tiny isle anchored to Anglesey's Holy Island (also known as Holyhead Island) by bridge. Here, you'll get one of the best sunsets over Cardigan Bay (**see p. 179** ☞) and, on a clear day, see the mainland's mountain ranges that make this area of Wales so special.

Don't forget: your car! Even though it's an island, you can drive over the Menai or Britannia Bridges and explore in your own set of wheels. This makes it a perfect place for a mini road trip or as part of a wider tour of North Wales.

How to get there: If you'd rather be a passenger, take the train to Holyhead on Holy Island, the ferry from Holyhead or the plane from Cardiff.

Verbose village

Anglesey is also home to the longest place name in all of Europe, the village of Llanfairpwllgwyngyllgogerychwyrn-drobwllllantysiliogogogoch. Yeah, it's a tongue-twister!

An island delight that Irish pirates, Romans, Vikings, English and even Norwegians loved!

Double-take Destinations

Places to surprise you

Great Britain is definitely full of surprises. Just when you think you have it all sussed out, this awesome island pulls another brilliant trick from its sleeve. Packed full of places that'll transport you to other areas of the world, this section's all about showcasing the very best in Great British gems.

Penbryn Beach
♀ CEREDIGION
Looks like: The Hamptons in New York

Gorgeous fine sands, incredible sunsets and cute little seaside villages close by, Penbryn Beach has a charm all of its own with a hint of that relaxed Hamptons aesthetic. Head out for a stroll on the beach, take a picnic and set up camp for a day by the dunes and a paddle in the surf.

Bude Sea Pool
♀ CORNWALL
Looks like: Bronte Baths, Australia

If you can block out the temperatures and lack of coral reef, this partially manmade sea pool bears a striking resemblance to the popular Australian swimming spot.

Tinwood Vineyard
♀ WEST SUSSEX
Looks like: Champagne, France

With a glass of Tinwood's own sparkling wine in hand, you'd be forgiven for thinking you were in the heart of Champagne. And with good reason, too! As it turns out, the grapes they use to make champagne do particularly well in West Sussex's soil. In fact, this part of England is becoming increasingly popular (and important) for English wines. Bubbles, anyone?

Elegug Stacks
♀ PEMBROKESHIRE
Looks like: Twelve Apostles, Australia

Those dramatic sea stacks look straight out of an Aussie soap opera, but they're right here on the lush Welsh coast. They're also not too far from the Green Bridge of Wales (*see* p. 102 ☞), so be sure to check that out, too.

Pentle Bay
♀ ISLES OF SCILLY
Looks like: The Caribbean

With its white sandy beaches, subtropical weather and clear blue waters, this Tresco beach could easily stand in for St Lucia or Barbados. You'll also find palm trees on the island – one of the few places in Britain it's warm enough for them to grow.

Cheddar Gorge
♀ SOMERSET
Looks like: The Inca Trail, Peru

Interested in the Inca Trail but not ready to commit? Enjoy traipsing through this limestone gorge in the Mendip Hills and avoid all the breathlessness that comes with high altitude.

Portmeirion
GWYNEDD
Looks like: Amalfi Coast, Italy

One of Britain's more successful 20th-century architectural projects, the village of Portmeirion in North Wales was built by Sir Clough Williams-Ellis. Perched overlooking the estuary of the River Dwyryd and styled around a Mediterranean piazza, it feels a world away from Wales. Be sure to check out some of that world-famous Portmeirion pottery, too.

Luskentyre Beach
ISLE OF HARRIS
Looks like: Cape Cod, Massachusetts

This northerly Scottish escape might be a little off the grid, but it's worth the trek for stunning white sand set against clear blue waters – when the sun's out, you could be summering at the Cape. And even on the sunniest day, you'll never be crammed in like sardines.

Fearnmore
SCOTTISH HIGHLANDS
Looks like: Western Norway

The Highlands landscape was shaped by many of the same Ice Age processes that created the stunning fjord landscapes in Norway. Take the coastal road from Applecross to Shieldaig (or vice versa) for views upon views upon views.

Minack Theatre
PORTHCURNO
Looks like: Athens, Greece

This open-air theatre, built into the side of the Cornish coast, might not be an Ancient Greek odeum, but it's no less impressive! Catch a play between spring and summer, or visit in the off season for a little nosey around. Just be sure to pack a jumper – Mediterranean heat isn't guaranteed.

St Michael's Mount
CORNWALL
Looks like: Mont-Saint-Michel, France

Situated in Mount's Bay off Southern England's coast, the tidal island of St Michael's Mount (*see p. 52* ☞) has a pretty similar vibe to its French sibling. They're both eye-catching, with impressive buildings perched on top and lots of history to discover.

Hitchin Lavender
HERTFORDSHIRE
Looks like: Provence, France

If you can't make it to southern France's famed lavender fields, there's a treasure-trove of the purple blooms growing in the home counties. Discover 35 miles of lavender – visit between mid-June and mid-August during the flowering season – and browse the shop for gifts.

Royal Pavilion
BRIGHTON
Looks like: Agra, India

Built in the Indo-Saracenic style more commonly seen in India, the Royal Pavilion (also known as the Brighton Pavilion) is a former palace with some serious Taj Mahal vibes. Inside this seaside pad, built for King George IV, you'll find lavish bedrooms, a banqueting hall and grand saloon.

Shetland Islands
SCOTLAND
Looks like: Iceland

These Scottish islands only look a tad like the very volcanic land of fire and ice, but head out at night to look for the Northern Lights and you'll start to feel like you're on a real Icelandic adventure. Dark, clear skies are best to view the Northern Lights, so visit from mid-October to mid-March for the best chance of seeing them.

Isle of Skye
INNER HEBRIDES
Looks like: Syðradalur, The Faroe Islands

Marvel at the dramatic and jagged landscape. Skye is such a gorgeous part of Scotland and has many of the features of its North Atlantic cousins. Be sure to spend some time exploring the Quiraing on the eastern face of Meall na Suiramach. The views are breathtaking.

Culture, Cafes and Cobbles

**Cities to inspire
and explore**

⬆ 'House hunting' in Wells

⬆ Finding hidden treasures in London's Natural History Museum

British cities are a brilliant smorgasbord of what makes our island so great. Having lived in multiple metropolises across the country, we've honed a strong sense of what to look out for and how to have the best time. Whether indulging in a short break or sampling the hustle and bustle as part of a bigger trip, visiting a city is a great way to sink your teeth into a local area. You'll get a sense of a region's culture and history at a much faster pace than you would if you ventured off into the countryside.

And speaking of history, there's lots to discover. So many of the cities we've chosen have hundreds of years of the stuff just waiting to be explored. Some are famous, attracting crowds from all over the world, but others are lesser known, more like regional secrets that you'll be pleasantly surprised to stumble upon.

We could list the many reasons why you should visit Great Britain's cities (incredible architecture, food, views, nightlife, etc.) but we'd be here all day. Instead, let's jump into our city selection box and get down to the nitty-gritty of why these picks make perfect places to visit. ♫

Top up that Oyster card and get exploring ...

London
♀ ENGLAND

London is one of those places that's a) an obvious choice to visit and b) got so much going on that it's tricky to know where to begin. If it's your first time in town, you should feel free to embrace the touristy sites. The British Museum, the London Eye, Big Ben, the Tower of London and the Queen's city pad (Buckingham Palace) – they're popular for a reason. Ignore travel elitists who turn their noses up at anyone wandering near the beaten path. Even as Londoners, we soak up the sights on a regular basis, especially when we have visitors staying.

There are some pretty amazing secret spots worth checking out, too. Like St Dunstan in the East Church Garden, an incredible church ruin that's hidden in plain sight right in the city centre. Or the smallest police station in the country tucked away in Trafalgar Square.

London neighbourhoods are experiences in themselves. They're nearly all worth dipping into. Spending a day strolling the markets in Notting Hill will feel nothing like heading to the more edgy area of Shoreditch or around Brick Lane, where you can grab an authentic Bangladeshi curry.

One thing we can guarantee is that you won't be able to 'do it all' in one trip to our capital city, and you'll constantly find reasons to return.

Edinburgh

📍 SCOTLAND

With thousands of years of history, a castle on top of an ancient volcanic butte and the picturesque Old Town, the Scottish capital is a beautiful way to experience a slice of Scotland.

It's a brilliant mix of old and new, with loads to keep you entertained the entire time you're there. It's also a stunner around sunrise or sunset. For amazing views, make sure to ramble your way up Arthur's Seat and see the city from up high.

If uphill hikes aren't your thing, pop over to Mary King's Close and head downhill instead. There, beneath the Royal Mile, you'll find an underground city that used to be part of Edinburgh but was sealed off during the plague and built over.

Fancy a dose of vibrant culture? Visit in August when the Edinburgh Festival Fringe is on. It's the world's largest arts festival, with tens of thousands of performances to choose from, so you'll be spoiled for choice. The Fringe culminates in an enormous firework display set to a live orchestra.

Auld Lang Syne

Another festival worth showing up for is Hogmanay (the New Year's festival). The city turns into a three-day party, capped off with fantastic fireworks on 31 December – it's one of the best ways to ring in the New Year.

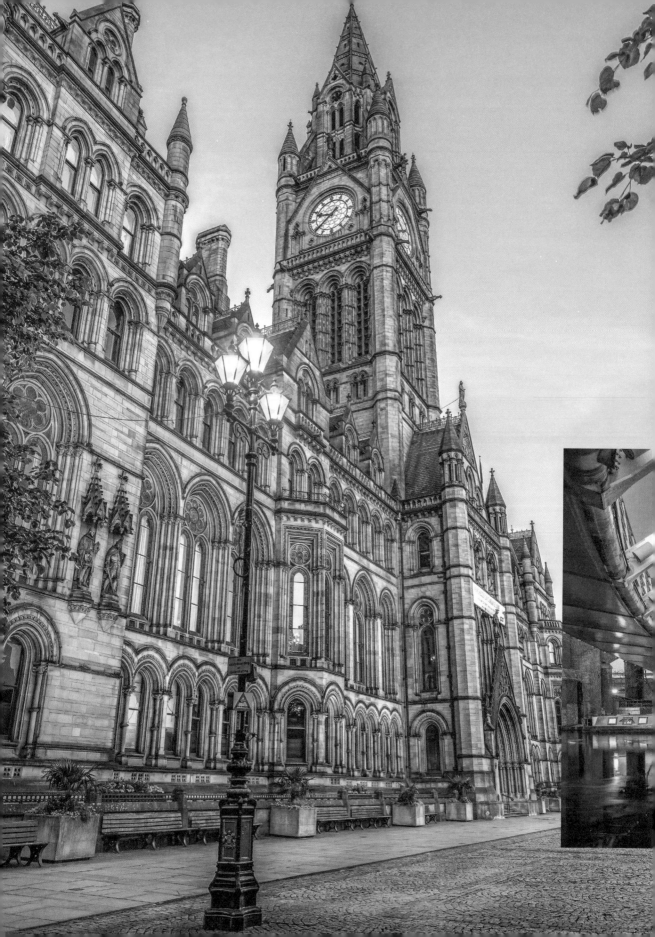

Manchester

♀ ENGLAND

Manchester was once at the heart of Britain's Industrial Revolution (hence, its symbolic association with bees – known for their tireless work ethic), but hard graft aside, this city knows how to party. It still holds an important place in Britain's rich musical tapestry, home to many celebrated musicians, including Oasis, The Smiths, The Stones Roses, and Take That.

There are historical sights aplenty, as well as exceptional museums and galleries, like The Whitworth and the Manchester Museum, to fill your time to the brim. We recommend stopping in at John Rylands Library (an architectural masterpiece both inside and outside), Manchester United's home Old Trafford (if you're a footie fan), the cathedral and the Manchester Art Gallery for a great selection of works by both local and international artists.

Good food and fun times
Tuck into Chinatown's host of yummy restaurants and then party the night away in one of the bars or clubs around Canal Street – the city's renowned LGBTQIA+ neighbourhood.

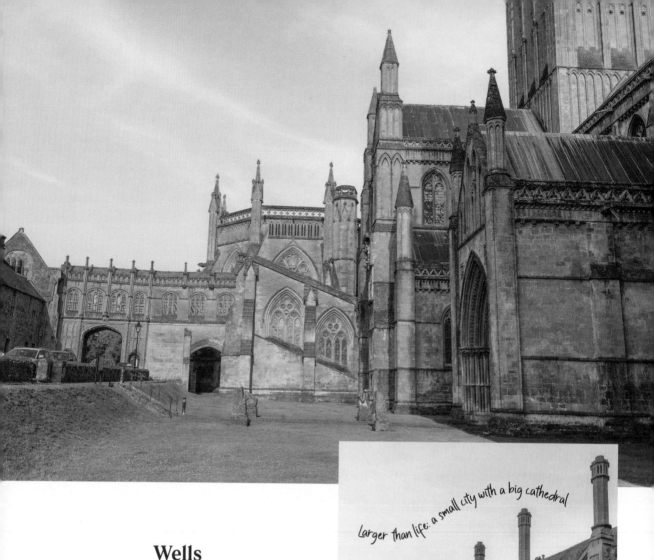

Larger than life: a small city with a big cathedral

Wells

♀ ENGLAND

Wells is the smallest city in England (fine, second smallest if you include the City of London) but it packs quite a punch. Named after the city's three wells, all dedicated to St Andrew, it's home to one of the country's most beautiful cathedrals, picturesque streets and quintessential English properties. Sights include the 12th-century Gothic cathedral, the medieval Bishop's Palace and Vicars' Close – one of the prettiest streets we've ever seen.

Wells is a relatively easy daytrip from London. Why not incorporate a trip to England's biggest city with a visit to its smallest – a cool humble brag to throw into conversation. Or tag it onto a wider road trip to include the many beautiful towns and villages of the Cotswolds (see p. 205 ☞) and the gorgeous Roman city of Bath (see p. 77 ☞).

Norwich

📍 **ENGLAND**

Norwich is home to some of the most beautiful lanes, squares and chocolate-box houses in all of England. We recommend starting your visit with the iconic Norwich Cathedral – walk through the Cloisters and take in the latest exhibition at the Hostry. When you're done, go wandering around the cobbles of Elm Hill, one of the prettiest Tudor streets in England, and be sure to visit the city's medieval castle, too.

Norwich has a thriving covered market, which has been in operation for over 900 years. It was key to making the city one of the largest and most prosperous in all of Great Britain. These days, you'll find a treasure trove of traders selling everything from vintage clothes to some of the most delicious food in the city.

Park life
Did you know that Norwich is the only city in England that's located inside a National Park? Positioned on the outer edge of the Broads, it's a gateway to explore Norfolk's waterways and coastline.

Glasgow

📍 SCOTLAND

Glasgow is Edinburgh's crazy (in a very good way), fun-fuelled sister! That's not to say that the city doesn't have refined culture or a serious side. Quite the opposite; it's a thriving hub chock-full of amazing history, an impressive arts scene and some incredible food. And because Glasgow is only 45 minutes by train from Edinburgh, if you're visiting from further afield, you can always check them both out as part of the same trip.

Be sure to visit Kelvingrove Art Gallery and Museum, home to one of the widest ranges of art collections and artefacts in Scotland; wander around George Square; and go see the Hunterian Art Gallery – the oldest public museum in Scotland. Then stop off at Pollok House to visit the stately home of Sir William Burrell (a Scottish shipping merchant with a penchant for antiquing) and peruse his incredible Spanish art collection.

If your timing is right, experience (or take part in!) the now world-famous annual Santa Dash, a festive charity run (or walk) through the city where everyone dresses up as Father Christmas.

Brighton

📍 ENGLAND

The ultimate British seaside city, laidback Brighton is just an hour from London by train, making it well connected to the rest of the country. We love how walkable the city is – you're never more than about 15 minutes away from any destination, making it easy to get to know, even if your time there is short.

It's pretty much obligatory to pay a visit to the Brighton Palace Pier, which has stood as a sentinel over the water for more than a century. There you can enjoy a few of the rides, grab some fish and chips and take a stroll along the wooden walkways.

Make sure to leave some time to explore The Lanes (see p. 163 ☞) – Brighton's eclectic shopping district. Pop into the little independent stores and grab yourself a few keepsakes. We loved BouSham Gallery for an eclectic collection of local art, and for a sweet treat, head over to Julien Plumart Boutique to pick up delicious macarons.

Royal splendour
If you love beautiful buildings, you'll find the Royal Pavilion (also known as the Brighton Pavilion) a short walk from the pier (see p. 59 ☞). This former royal residence dates back to the 18th century and will surprise you at every turn.

Filled with riverside walks, Roman baths and baked-fresh buns!

Bath
♀ ENGLAND

Nestled in the South West of England, Bath is an ancient Roman spa town – known for its natural hot springs. The centre has been heavily protected by law against any changes, meaning the character, charm and iconic Bath stone buildings have been preserved for centuries for us to enjoy today.

The first thing you have to do when you visit is head over to the Roman Baths. After all, it's where the city's name comes from – not to mention one of the most incredible sights. Once you've stepped back in time at the ancient baths, head over to the Thermae Bath Spa – the only natural thermal spa in Britain – for a chance to relax just like the Romans did (only with the added luxury of an open-air rooftop pool).

Other spots to sate your inner historian include the Royal Crescent, the Abbey and the Circus (think, fewer acrobats and more townhouses – it's a very pretty ring-shaped street). Or visit the Jane Austen Centre to learn more about the life and work of this one-time Bath resident.

Lunn's bunns

After you've built up an appetite, stop in at Sally Lunn's – one of the oldest houses in Bath – to try their 'bunns' (a part-bread, part-cake Bath delicacy)!

Bristol

♀ ENGLAND

Bristol is famous for its art scene – one of the best reasons to visit, especially for work by one of its more famous residents: Banksy. You'll find the elusive street artist's work dotted across the city (check out visitbristol.co.uk for a self-guided walking tour to take in some of his most iconic pieces).

Some of the other interesting museums and art galleries to check out include The Bristol Museum and Art Gallery – an extensive collection of local art and artefacts spanning natural history, archaeology and geology; M Shed to explore Bristol's history; and Brunel's SS *Great Britain*, a ship-come-museum that takes you back to the mid-1800s when it was used for crossings to New York.

For city views, head up to the Clifton Suspension Bridge, pop into Bristol Cathedral and go for a stroll around the Harbourside. Stop at Spike Island's Wapping Wharf to while away the afternoon by the River Avon. There are some great art spaces, restaurants and boutique shops to explore. Once you've had your fill of Bristol, make a beeline for Bath – less than 15 minutes away by train.

Don't count on spotting Banksy – his identity is still unknown!

Hand Luggage Only

St Davids

♀ WALES

St Davids in Pembrokeshire is the smallest city in Great Britain – even smaller than Wells (see p. 68 ☞) but equally charming. In the historical heart of the city is the cathedral, built in 1181, but the holy history of the site started centuries before. Its popularity as a centre of pilgrimage began after William the Conqueror visited almost 1000 years ago.

The cathedral towers over the rest of St Davids. Stroll around the grounds, then head inside and see the renovated cloisters and stunning organ. Don't forget to visit the Bishop's Palace right next door on the other side of the River Alun. There are a number of cute restaurants, pubs and shops in the city, so set aside some time for a leisurely amble and lunch (we ate fresh and tasty fish and chips at Peter's Plaice). Staying the night? Make dinner reservations at the St Davids Cross Hotel Bar & Restaurant.

Cardiff

Wales's capital has heaps of history, culture and lots to see and do – perfect for a weekend away.

We couldn't get enough of Cardiff Castle. From the outside it's pretty impressive, but wait till you get through the door. There you'll find intricately designed halls, gilded rooms and the Arab Room – a beautiful Moorish inspired space, complete with ornate golden high-vaulted ceilings.

If you can, catch a play at Wales Millennium Centre and pop into the National Museum for contemporary art and natural history – the Evolution of Wales exhibition is particularly good.

One of the best ways to truly enjoy Cardiff is with a night on the town. It's raucous, hilarious and amazing all at once! Oh, and before you leave, do be sure to stock up on lots of Welsh cakes.

Cambridge

♀ ENGLAND

Cambridge is one of the most beautiful cities in England. Take a wander around the stunning grounds of the famous university – the colleges are a key part of what makes Cambridge so special. You can visit them all, though some charge an entry fee (Clare, Corpus Christi, St John's, King's, Queens' and Trinity Colleges) – all of which are really worth the cost. King's College chapel is a must-see. Look out for the striking wooden rood screen – the partition between the chancel and the nave. It was gifted by Henry VIII (the one who had six wives) to Anne Boleyn (one of the wives who ended up beheaded).

You can't visit Cambridge without hiring a punt – a flat-bottomed boat that you propel along with the help of a long pole. It's pretty hard work, so you can always pay a professional to do it for you. And if you're feeling really fit, see the views from the church tower at Great St Mary's. You'll be rewarded with one of the best vistas over the city. Be warned, though, the historic stone tower shakes quite a bit when the bells are ringing.

Cambridge through and through

As previous residents of this amazing city (Yaya's a graduate of its world-famous university), we should say we're completely biased about Cambridge. In that infamous rivalry with Oxford, our loyalties definitely lie with our former home! You can catch a coach between the two if you want to compare for yourself, though.

Oxford
📍 ENGLAND

The perfect city to explore by foot or punt!

Despite being big fans of our alma mater, we'd be remiss not to mention Oxford on this list (after all, Cambridge University was founded as an off-shoot of Oxford 800 years ago). The city centres around the university – the most recognisable college is Christ Church. If it looks familiar, that's because it stands in for a number of Hogwarts locations in the Harry Potter films.

You can punt in Oxford on the River Cherwell, which takes you past a number of the university's beautiful colleges.

If you're not sure where to begin once you arrive in the city, a good place is at the Radcliffe Camera (which, despite what the name might suggest, is actually a library). From there you'll find yourself within walking distance of some of the city's most iconic spots, including the Bodleian Library, Hertford Bridge (known as the Bridge of Sighs for its similar appearance to the real deal in Venice), The Queen's College and Brasenose College, to mention a few.

York

📍 ENGLAND

It only took a day of exploring York for us to start scouring property websites, such is its lure. While it's one of the oldest cities in Britain (there's evidence of people living there dating back to at least 7000 BCE), it never gets old! There's always something new to explore, see and experience. A great way to get your bearings is by following the 14th-century walls that enclose the medieval city, stopping off at the little boutiques en route.

Don't forget to pop into the impressive York Minster, the largest Gothic building in Britain, and the National Railway Museum, where you'll find trains from all over the world, including a few once ridden by the Royal family – it's a trainspotter's dream.

Then take a stroll down The Shambles, a higgledy-piggledy street with serious olde England vibes. You'll feel like you've stepped back in time (or into a Harry Potter film – rumour has it that this spot was the real-life inspiration for Diagon Alley).

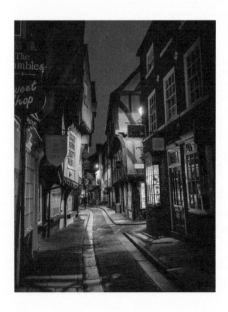

A Nordic name

The name York comes from the Vikings, who renamed it Jorvik when they settled there in 866 CE. For a more in-depth look at the city's Nordic heritage, including reconstructions of Viking-era streets (smells included!), check out the Jorvik Viking Centre.

Aberdeen

⚲ SCOTLAND

Aberdeen might look grey, thanks to the local granite most of the city is constructed with, but it's got a lot of charm too. And its distinctly different feel to other Scottish cities makes it worth the trip. Our favourite sights include the Gothic revivalist grandeur of Marischal College – you'll struggle to find a similar building elsewhere in Britain – and Brig o'Balgownie, the oldest bridge in Scotland.

Get up close and personal with the medieval penal system at the Tolbooth Museum. This crime and punishment attraction is housed in one of the city's oldest buildings, and you can even visit the original prison cells from the 1600s.

Aberdeenshire is a beautiful part of Scotland, so while you're in the area, make a beeline for Dunnottar, Crathes and Craigievar Castles and dip into the many cute Scottish towns and villages dotted around the wild countryside.

Lincoln

📍 ENGLAND

Lincoln might not be on most people's British city bucket list, but we think it should be. Sleepier than some of the other spots we've recommended, it's a beautiful place to while away the weekend. It's got picturesque streets galore and the imposing Lincoln Cathedral (the tallest building in the world for some 200 years).

Strap on those walking shoes and go explore Steep Hill with its lovely little shops and houses (and an impressive 16.12° gradient). For a bite to eat, pop into Rising Café – a favourite spot with the locals serving up delicious food – just be sure to bring your appetite with you! For a deeper insight into the region, pop into the Museum of Lincolnshire Life. Lincoln's not that big, so you can wander at your leisure without worrying about getting lost.

Falls, Cliffs and Caves

Natural wonders
to blow your mind

↑ Zig-zagging through Bealach na Bà in the Scottish Highlands

The history of Great Britain is famous the world over. What's perhaps not as well known, however, is its varied geography. But it would be a huge mistake to overlook the incredible natural wonders to be found here. There's so much to see, with several of Britain's incredible natural sights easily being some of the most impressive in Europe and, arguably, across the world.

From rugged limestone formations and colossal chalky cliffs to verdant green lochs and jaw-dropping waterfalls, you just need to know where to look.

In this chapter, we'll follow forest trails that unveil unexpected delights, traverse coastal paths where you won't get far without taking a photo and stop along stretches of road that deliver view after unspoiled view.

These natural beauties also offer the perfect excuse to get your walking boots on and make the most of the Great British outdoors. So, what are you waiting for? Camera at the ready, it's time to embrace nature (and possibly get a little damp). 🥾

Winnats Pass

📍 **ENGLAND**

Winnats Pass is a limestone gorge in the Peak District with stunning views. It's another natural sight that can easily be marvelled at from the comfort of your car but is best appreciated on foot. Once you're done wandering around the area, make some time to pop into Speedwell Cavern, a beautiful limestone cave, which is hidden in plain sight at the mouth of Winnats Pass. To get in, you go down 105 steps in a miner's shaft. Don't worry, it's not as tight as it sounds, but it's not suitable for wheelchair users. At the bottom you catch a boat that takes you along the underground canal of a 200-year-old lead mine and into vast caverns that you can explore.

Durdle Door

9 ENGLAND

This incredible natural arch found on Dorset's Jurassic Coast is one of the most popular places for holidaymakers to visit in the area, and it's not hard to see why. Eroded by the waves thrashing at England's shores, this limestone formation has been carved into an iconic arch. Eventually the arch will collapse into the sea, but for now, you can enjoy it in all its glory. Set right on the beach, it makes for a stunning backdrop for your day of fun in the sun. If you want to skip the crowds, however, visit in late spring or early autumn when there are fewer tourists to ruin your photos.

While you're here, explore the coastline. You'll find more unique geology at Lulworth Cove, seafood galore at the old fishing port of Swanage and award-winning beaches at Studland Bay – all within easy reach.

Eroded by the waves thrashing at England's shores

Cheddar Gorge
📍 ENGLAND

The first thing that strikes you as you make your way through Cheddar Gorge is how huge it is. Situated on the southern edge of Somerset's Mendip Hills, this limestone marvel is one of the most important natural sites in England. The best way to explore the area is by foot. Wander through the gorge on a hike or, for the more adventurous visitor, there's abseiling, caving or rock climbing here. If ever there was a place to get your adrenaline pumping, this is it.

The gorge is just up the road from the village of Cheddar, famous for – you guessed it – its much-loved cheese. You absolutely need to 'gorge' on some cheddar cheese while you're there. We recommend the Cheddar Gorge Cheese Company and The Original Cheddar Cheese Company, where they've been making delicious cheeses since 1870.

Cheesed off

Cheddar is where the oldest complete human skeleton found in Britain was discovered. Known as the Cheddar man, DNA analysis suggests he probably had green eyes, dark curly hair and very dark skin. He was also lactose intolerant, so no Cheddar cheese for him.

Malham Cove

♀ ENGLAND

If you're visiting the Yorkshire Dales National Park (**see p. 156** ☞), don't miss out on Malham Cove – a curved limestone rock formation, created by a powerful glacial waterfall at the end of the last Ice Age. There's no waterfall now, but it's no less impressive. This thing is big – the cliff's vertical face is about 260 feet (80 metres), which makes it a popular spot for experienced rock climbers. If you are keen to climb here, it's probably best to pick a cloudy day. The cliff is south-facing and as a result can get incredibly hot in the sunshine. With well-maintained paths at the top and bottom, it's worth the walk up to get the best of both viewpoints.

If it looks familiar, there's good reason – the cove has been the backdrop of quite a few TV shows and films, including *Harry Potter and the Deathly Hallows: Part 1* and *Wuthering Heights*.

Pistyll Rhaeadr

📍 **WALES**

Widely regarded as the tallest waterfall in Wales, split over three levels, Pistyll Rhaeadr is one of the country's most breathtaking sights. You'll find it in Powys, not too far from (and good luck pronouncing this if you're not Welsh) Llanrhaeadr-ym-Mochnant. With its staggering height of 240 feet (73 metres) and bridge jutting out over the middle, you'll feel like you're in Middle Earth from *The Lord of the Rings*. If ever there was a place to appreciate how much it rains in Wales, this is it.

The surrounding area is also great for hiking, so when you're done with the waterfall, explore more of Wales's natural beauty on one of the nearby trails. It's important to note that it is a Site of Special Scientific Interest, meaning it's protected. So keep your eyes peeled for interesting wildlife, and take care to leave the area as pristine as you found it.

Seven Sisters

📍 **ENGLAND**

Arguably one of the most iconic sights of the Great British coastline, Seven Sisters in the South Downs National Park is one of the best places to spend a summer's afternoon, although the sheer sight of the cliffs makes it an impressive place to visit anytime.

The cliffs here remain white as they're constantly eroding, revealing new layers of sedimentary chalk limestone. Suffice to say, it makes for quite the stunning sight.

Walking is the order of the day. It's hard to get lost here (you're literally following the cliff edge), so feel free to plod along at your leisure. There's a visitor centre when you arrive, with toilets and information on walking. Remember, the cliffs can crumble very easily without warning, so never walk right on the edge.

The Green Bridge

📍 WALES

Not too far from Pembroke (and its incredible castle) lies the Green Bridge of Wales. Similar to Durdle Door (**see p. 97** ☞) in England, the Green Bridge is a huge limestone arch set in Wales's jagged coastline. Less popular, and therefore less busy, than some of the other sights listed here, it's well worth a visit. Look out for the viewing platform to properly take in the beauty of this arch. After getting your fill, enjoy a walk east from here to see other pretty spots like the Elegug Stacks, The Cauldron and Flimston Bay.

The Needles

📍 ISLE OF WIGHT

The Needles are three dramatic chalk stacks jutting out of the sea on the edge of the island. The Isle of Wight is brilliant in the summer, but if you do come on a blustery day, with rolling clouds and crashing waves, the Needles can look even more impressive. Be warned: they don't actually look like needles – they get their name from a fourth stack, which collapsed into the ocean centuries ago. See them from the Old Battery (a Victorian fort owned by the National Trust) or at Alum Bay. Take the chair lift down to the beach below or get up close with a boat trip (available from Easter till late October, weather permitting), where you truly get a sense of how huge they are.

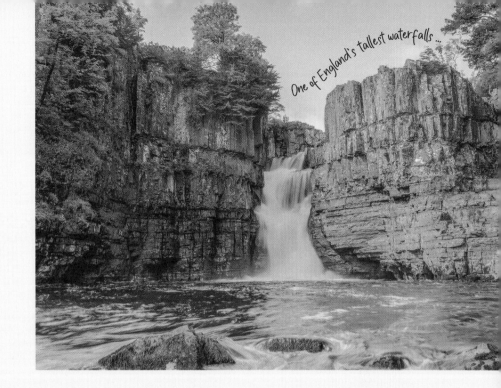

High Force

📍 **ENGLAND**

The name for this waterfall is so apt, as it really is an incredible force of nature. Located in the North Pennines, it looks like it belongs in a tropical jungle rather than on the border of Yorkshire and County Durham. It's one of the highest waterfalls in England, dating back 300 million years, and most spectacular in the winter months. To make your way there, park up at Bowlees Visitor Centre, and take a gorgeous walk through the forest (nothing too strenuous). In cold conditions, the waterfall's been known to freeze, making for a spectacular sight more at home in northern Canada.

Force of nature
High Force isn't all about the water. It's surrounded by some fantastic wildlife, too – look out for deer, rabbits and other critters when you visit.

An Lochan Uaine

♀ SCOTLAND

We first found out about An Lochan Uaine (The Green Lochan) at the start of a road trip through the Scottish Highlands. Legend has it that its unique colour comes from Dòmhnall Mòr, the king of the pixies, washing his clothes in the lake. Science, on the other hand, says that rotting wood on the lake floor creates algae that turns the water green.

To see it for yourself, park near the Glenmore Forest Park Visitor Centre and walk from there (past the Glenmore Lodge). At around 40 minutes each way, it's a fairly easy walk, taking you past rolling heather-covered hills and the occasional bunny rabbit. Or follow our lead and rent a couple of bicycles from In Your Element over at the Rothiemurchus Pavilion – they've got helmets and bike trailers for little ones, too.

Bealach na Bà

♀ SCOTLAND

Bealach na Bà is considered by many as one of the most beautiful roads in the world and they're not wrong. Now the name might refer to a road, but you're not here for the tarmac – you're here for the absolutely gorgeous nature that surrounds it. Bealach na Bà takes you through an incredible part of the Scottish Highlands, where natural wonders can be seen in all directions. From this single-track pass you can survey the beautiful swathe of valley, carved out by a glacier thousands of years ago, all the way down to the nearby Loch Kishorn.

The views here are best teamed with a road trip through the Highlands, including the towns and villages of Applecross, Plockton (*see* p. 180 ☞) and Shieldaig, to mention a few, and historic gems like Eilean Donan Castle (*see* p. 23 ☞).

Driver beware

If you're not a confident driver, you might want to give this a miss. As the road climbs to a height of 2053 feet (626 metres) it gets pretty narrow at points, and you'll need to be prepared to stop and allow oncoming traffic to pass.

Tuck in

Gorgeous grub to get your mitts on

The best way to these travellers' hearts is through our tummies. Great food brings our towns, cities and remote locales to life, and makes them unique. From Michelin Star spots to local chippies, we've tried and tested this bulging menu of morsels for quality, atmosphere and downright deliciousness. These are places where the food not only tastes great but that are experiences in their own right. It might be the atmosphere, the friendly chefs or seasonal menu or a combination of all the above.

For the best of British:
Hawksmoor Borough
♀ LONDON

A meat-lover's dream! Hawksmoor is an award-winning steakhouse that has one of the best cast-iron fillet steaks in all the land. Hawsksmoor prides itself on serving the best cuts from small British farmers. If you visit on a Sunday, reserve a table for their slow roast rump finished off with lashings of bone marrow and onion gravy.

16 Winchester Walk, London

(More Hawksmoor restaurants can be found elsewhere in London, and in Manchester and Edinburgh.)

For the seasonal menus:
Roots York
♀ YORK

Roots is world-class and adopts seasonal menus that follow three growing groups: The Preserving Season, The Hunger Gap and The Time of Abundance. The menu is constantly evolving to mirror what becomes available from the restaurant's own farm. Just be sure to make a reservation on the weekend!

68 Marygate, York

For fine dining:
The Witchery by the Castle
📍 **EDINBURGH**

Nestled on the historic Royal Mile, the Witchery by the Castle is an Edinburgh institution – people have been dining here for over 50 years. The restaurant is lined with sumptuous oak panelling and bathed in candlelight. It's a legendary fine-dining experience with a magical atmosphere.

352 Castlehill, Edinburgh

For proudly Welsh dishes:
Harbourmaster
📍 **ABERAERON**

Serving freshly caught seafood from the well-stocked larder of West Wales's Cardigan Bay, the Harbourmaster is proudly Welsh and totally delicious. The crab is so yummy, and they've got a great list of award-winning ales and gin to wash it down with.

Pen Cei, Aberaeron, Ceredigion

For chips with a twist:
Grosvenor Fish Bar
📍 **NORWICH**

As one of the best fish and chip shops in England, the Grosvenor Fish Bar has made something of a name for itself over the last 90 years. Filled with the firm favourites you'd come to expect from a tasty chippie, they also mix up house-made condiments like wasabi mayo, bang bang sauce (for an added kick) and minted lemon mayo.

28 Lower Goat Ln, Norwich

For the lobster:
The Potted Lobster
📍 **BAMBURGH**

Any guesses what this place is good for? With a totally rustic feel, The Potted Lobster serves up these tasty crustaceans from Northumberland's local shores. Each lobster comes either poached, cold or grilled, depending on the sauces you pick. You won't be disappointed.

3 Lucker Rd, Bamburgh

For the brunch:
Fitzbillies
📍 **CAMBRIDGE**

In the business of baking since 1920, Fitzbillies knows what it's doing when it comes to brunch. Popular with Cambridge University students, the cafe on Bridge Street serves up tasty muffin stacks, mouth-watering Chelsea buns and some of the finest seasonal treats in all of Cambridgeshire.

36 Bridge St and 51–52 Trumpington St, Cambridge

For the Welsh cakes:
Cardiff Bakestones
📍 **CARDIFF**

Bursting with freshly baked goodies, right within Cardiff's bustling Market Hall, Bakestones makes Welsh cakes the old-fashioned way – on a traditional hot griddle, right before your eyes. If you've never had one, you haven't truly lived. These sweet, griddled cakes are typically filled with sultanas and best served warm with a nice cuppa. Just make sure you buy more than one.

Cardiff Market, 49 St Mary St, Cardiff

For the oysters:
Wheelers Oyster Bar
📍 WHITSTABLE

Founded over 150 years ago, Wheelers Oyster Bar is a Whitstable mainstay. From the outset, Wheelers has sourced the freshest seafood and makes everything else from scratch: the bread, ice cream, you name it! Order the super-fresh rocky oysters for a special treat. Don't fret if you're not into shellfish: they have a range of locally sourced fresh fish, too.

8 High St, Whitstable

For a tasting menu:
The Cellar
📍 ANSTRUTHER

This quaint and cosy restaurant, set in a historic Fife fishing village overlooking the North Sea, offers a flavourful Scottish tasting menu. Typically around six courses, it's a fine-dining experience unexpected of a small coastal town. With dishes featuring ingredients like smoked haddock, venison and poached turnip, your taste buds will be spoilt rotten.

24 E Green, Anstruther

For a plant-based treat:
Farmacy
📍 LONDON

Notting Hill's Farmacy grows its own vegetables on a farm in Kent and transports them to the restaurant by electric van. The 100 per cent vegan menu is packed with the most scrummy plant-based dishes in London. Their earth bowls are especially tasty.

74–76 Westbourne Grove, London

For a Sunday roast:
Brassica
📍 BEAMINSTER

Around 20 minutes from the Jurassic Coast, Brassica is the perfect Dorset stop-off for a proper Sunday roast with all the trimmings. This award-winning haunt is popular with locals and visitors alike, so be sure to book ahead. You won't want to miss the Yorkshire puds!

4 The Square, Beaminster

For the award-winning dishes:
Estbeck House
📍 WHITBY

Just a few minutes' drive from the centre of Whitby, Estbeck House is the Yorkshire coast's very first two AA Rosette restaurant. One of the things that we love most about Estbeck House is how unstuffy and friendly it is. Just be sure to try some of their delicious ice cream, with a fantastic flavour list that includes everything from liquorice to ginger.

East Row, Whitby

For the comfort food:
Gille Brighde
📍 LOWER DIABAIG

Nestled on the shores of Loch Torridon, Gille Brighde is a cosy family-run Highlands restaurant that focuses on tasty comfort food, like their hearty seafood chowder, which warms you to your bones. You'll feel right at home – they'll even pop a few logs on the burner on colder days. Ask for a table overlooking the loch while you dine.

The Old Schoolhouse, Lower Diabaig, Torridon, Achnasheen

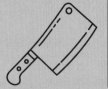

For a centuries-old watering hole:
Hare & Hounds

📍 **COWBRIDGE**

With over 300 years of pint pulling under its belt, this well-loved pub prides itself on serving the very best Welsh dishes. From freshly caught Gower mussels and roast wood pigeon to pheasant pies, the menu changes daily in line with what's available from local Vale producers.

Maendy Rd, Aberthin, Cowbridge

For the jerk:
Gidi Grill

📍 **DUNDEE**

On the banks of City Quay, near the River Tay, Gidi Grill was one of the tastiest surprises during our trip to Dundee. They make Caribbean and West African cuisine with a unique British twist (hello yummy jollof rice!). We lived for the reggae basket filled with spicy chicken, jerk sausages and jicama slaw.

1b Camperdown St, Dundee

To gorge on gelato:
Gelato Gusto

📍 **BRIGHTON**

You might be on the south coast of England, but the gelato here rivals any in Italy. Owner Jon Adams trained at Bologna's University of Gelato, so he knows his stuff. The team makes over 20 different flavours that change daily, including dairy-free. We can't get enough of the sea salt caramel.

2 Gardner St, Brighton

For the hoppers:
The Coconut Tree

📍 **BRISTOL**

Bringing a taste of Sri Lanka to Bristol, this spot serves up freshly prepared goat curry and kottu (with chopped roti, mountains of spices and veggies). Though, for us, it's all about the hoppers. We ate these bowl-shaped pancakes religiously in Sri Lanka and The Coconut Tree's took us right back. Order yours with egg and spicy lunumiris sauce.

237–239 Cheltenham Rd, Bristol

(More Coconut Tree restaurants can be found elsewhere in Bristol, and in Bournemouth, Cardiff, Cheltenham and Oxford.)

For a spicy sensation:
Dishoom Covent Garden

📍 **LONDON**

Influenced by the Irani Cafes of bustling Bombay, Dishoom is a flavourful trip not to be missed, with everything from chicken ruby and jackfruit biryani to keema pau (buttered buns and spicy minced lamb). The menu caters for gluten-free, dairy-free and vegan diners. Don't forget to try the Dishoom IPA, lovingly made by London's Mondo Brewing Company.

12 Upper St Martin's Ln, London

(More Dishoom restaurants can be found elsewhere in London, and in Manchester, Birmingham and Edinburgh.)

Sand Between
Your Toes

Brilliant beaches
worth the surf

Us Brits love a good beach. Regardless of where you are in Great Britain, you're never much further than 70 miles (112 kilometres) from the surf. This means that day trips, weekend breaks and cosy seaside retreats are easy-peasy, regardless of where you live or where you're staying.

First off, let's get past those bygone ideas that our beaches are painfully rocky and brimming with chip-stealing seagulls. Yes, we have those, too, but that notion is far from the unspoilt gems that we know and love. From hidden coves to vast sandy stretches, you're really spoilt for choice.

This is exactly why we want to show off some of our favourite, lesser-known spots. Prepare to soak up Balinese vibes, with a little sprinkle of Great British charm (and the odd stick of rock).

So, what are you waiting for? Grab yourself a towel, slap on that sunblock and head for the beach. Who needs Bali, eh? 🏄

Tresaith Beach

♀ WALES

Tiny Tresaith on Wales's western coast is made up of around 30 cottages and a local watering hole for drinks and dinner, but that's what makes it even more special. It's almost untouched and quite often missed by people unfamiliar with the area.

In the summer months, lifeguards patrol the beach – it's perfect for swimming on a calm day. Plus, as it's west facing, you get some of the most incredible sunsets. This region of Wales is known for them! After burying your best mate on the sandy shoreline, head to the northerly cliffs that tower over Tresaith Beach. That's where the rock pools begin. After a little crab spotting, keep walking – around 165 feet (50 metres) – where you'll find one of West Wales's most gorgeous waterfalls spilling out from the cliff, right into the sea below. When the tide is fully out, you can walk right up to the falls. It's like something out of *Jurassic Park*.

One of West Wales's most gorgeous waterfalls!

Spot the swimmers
Keep your eyes peeled for dolphins jumping out of the water. Cardigan Bay has the largest bottlenose dolphin population in Europe – more than 250 of them! Spot them from the coast or, if you fancy a closer look, head over to nearby New Quay (25 minutes in the car) and hop on a dolphin-spotting cruise (departing from the pier in the summer).

Ynyslas

📍 WALES

Just north of Aberystwyth (around a 25-minute drive away), Ynyslas is a sandy paradise that makes up the mouth of the Dyfi Valley. Here, you'll find protected sand dunes, wooden walkways and the finest sandy beach that stretches for miles.

On a calm day when the tide is out, you might be able to see a forest of prehistoric tree trunks emerging from the sea. Thousands of years ago, this whole area was a vast woodland until the water gobbled it up.

Make sure to bring all your Welsh cakes, bara brith (a tasty Welsh fruit loaf) and drinks with you. There are no shops or restaurants here, just stunning natural sites.

Learn the lingo
In Welsh, 'traeth' is the word for beach. If you see a sign for 'Traeth', head there!

Blue Lagoon
📍 WALES

Nestled on the Pembrokeshire coastline at Abereiddy Bay, the Blue Lagoon might not have oodles of sand (or typically be classed as a beach), but what it lacks in grains, it gains in gigantic rocks.

This historic quarry, now flooded with seawater, is a great place for paddling, diving or coasteering. Be sure to book a tour with a qualified guide like Celtic Quest Coasteering. If you're in the area and it's sand you're after, head further down the Pembrokeshire Coast Path (see p. 3 ☞) and visit Whitesands Bay.

For the adrenaline junkies
Blue Lagoon is known for its diving competitions, such as the Red Bull Cliff Diving World Series, which make it an even more exciting spot to visit.

Pembrokeshire has a heap of coastal coves to discover!

Bamburgh Beach
📍 ENGLAND

Although Northumberland is typically known as 'Castle County', it's also got a heap of captivating beaches that can't be missed. And Bamburgh is just that. With a vast stretch of unspoilt coastline, it's the perfect place to chill for a day in the dunes and surf. Although it never feels overcrowded (it's too big for that), if you want even more tranquillity, head to the south section of the beach.

West Sands

♀ SCOTLAND

Nestled next to the world's oldest golf course in St Andrews, West Sands is probably one of the best stretches of golden grains in all of Fife. Spanning nearly two miles (3.2 kilometres), it's a totally pristine beach, perfect for strolling and paddling on a Scottish summer day. That being said, even in the chills of winter, this beach is special! We've walked along it hundreds of times while studying in St Andrews. It never fails to impress us, especially when you see the town's historic buildings in the distance.

Pack layers: it's beautiful but sometimes a little bit blustery!

Don't forget to duck
Listen out for golfers shouting 'Fore!' This means a golf ball is likely to hit you – ouch! – so cover your head and keep your wits about you. even more exciting spot to visit.

Watergate Bay
♀ ENGLAND

Much quieter than the likes of nearby
Cornish Mecca Newquay, Watergate Bay
is known for its sandy shore and great
surf. Why not take it in as part of a hike on
the South West Coast Path (*see* p. 10 ☞).
Or you could stay the night at the nearby
Watergate Bay Hotel. With a contemporary
beach vibe, it's the kind of place that
encourages salty hair, sandy feet and full
tummies (especially with their breakfast
waffles). To test your skills on the waves,
book some lessons with the gang at
Extreme Academy. They'll have you
surfing like a pro in no time.

Camber Sands

📍 ENGLAND

Camber Sands is a pretty popular spot with locals and Londoners. This sandy escape runs for miles along the East Sussex coast. You can easily while away an afternoon relaxing in the dunes or keeping an eye out for local wildlife, like short-eared owls or hen harriers, which have been sighted wintering there in the colder months. Be sure to pack a picnic filled with treats – food choices can be limited and there's nothing worse than being hungry on the beach.

Sleep beneath the sails

Partner your trip to Camber Sands with an overnight stay at the Grade-II-listed Rye Windmill B&B (ryewindmill.co.uk) in the lovely little town of Rye (see p. 175 ☞). The Windmill Suite is our favourite.

Man O' War Beach

♀ ENGLAND

Trust us, Man O' War Beach is not quite as scary as it sounds! Perched on the beautiful Dorset coastline, just east of Durdle Door, it's part of the Jurassic Coast World Heritage Site, where you can head out fossil hunting **(see p. 202 ☞)**. With a mix of sand and fine shingles, it's a lovely place to relax with a good book.

At certain times of the year, the steps to Man O' War Beach are closed because of rough conditions or loose rocks. Check the situation before you go at visit-dorset. com, and don't attempt the descent against advice. Because of the steps, access will be tricky for some visitors. And be sure to grab everything from your car in one trip – to avoid repeated hikes back up all those steps.

It's rich pickings when it comes to blissful beaches on the south coast

Balnakeil Beach
📍 SCOTLAND

Situated just off the main A838 Road at Durness, in the north of Scotland, Balnakeil Beach is a remote idyll that could easily stand in for a deserted island film location. Without any vast developments (except the ruins of Balnakeil Church), this place is totally untouched.

You can easily spend a long afternoon here and a night or two at nearby Sango Sands, where you'll find a few cosy guesthouses and rental cottages. Why not make the journey as part of the North Coast 500 road trip (*see* p. 198 ☞).

St Agnes and Gugh
📍 ISLES OF SCILLY

The tiny islands of St Agnes and Gugh make up part of the Isles of Scilly, positioned around 25 miles (40 kilometres) off the coast of Cornwall. This whole iconic archipelago is renowned for its pristine beaches, but our favourite is the white sand bar that connects these two islands at low tide. Get there by hopping on a small passenger boat from Hugh Town on nearby St Mary's Island, taking around 15 minutes. Then, after having your fill of sun, sea and sand, stroll around St Agnes's country lanes – there's a lovely little cafe and a tiny pub, too.

Nippy dip
As the bay of Balnakeil Beach faces west, it's somewhat sheltered from the choppier seas. This means you're guaranteed some epic opportunities to take a dip on a calm day. It can be a little chilly, so pack a thermos to warm up afterwards!

Garry Beach (Traigh Ghearadha)

⚲ ISLE OF LEWIS

Nestled on the coastline of Scotland's Isle of Lewis (**see p. 42** ☞), Garry Beach is nearly 6 miles (10 kilometres) north of Gress. It's the perfect place to kick back, enjoy a slice of secluded paradise and marvel at the imposing sea stacks.

You'll probably want a car to explore (or calves of steel to cycle) to the more northerly points on the island, and Garry Beach is no exception. That being said, pack your walking boots, because there are some gorgeous trails that surround the beach and coastline.

Plan, plan, plan
The Isle of Lewis isn't the kind of place you can easily visit on a whim. We recommend booking the 2-hour 45-minute ferry ride from Ullapool to Stornoway in advance (calmac.co.uk). Petrol stations can also be few and far between on the island, so make sure you've always got a decent amount of fuel in the tank when you head out on a longer drive.

Camusdarach Beach
📍 SCOTLAND

Overlooking the island of Rùm in the Scottish Highlands, Camusdarach Beach might be a little off the beaten track, but it's totally worth the journey. In truth, you'd have no idea the beach was here if someone didn't tell you, as it's so secluded and tucked away.

The car park is about a 15-minute stroll away from the beach. You make your way along tiny trails surrounded by long grass before being greeted with the finest white sand and crystal-clear water. On a warm, sunny day, you'll feel like you've teleported yourself to the Caribbean ... it's that beautiful! As you approach the beach, drive slowly and keep your eyes peeled for the car park, signposted with a tiny blue 'P'. It's not obvious and is easy to miss.

Luskentyre Sands
📍 ISLE OF HARRIS

When we think of world-class beaches, it's hard not to imagine far-flung locales like the Maldives or Tahiti. But this jaw-dropping gem is much closer to home: Scotland's Isle of Harris (part of the same Hebridean island as the Isle of Lewis). Overlooking nearby Taransay, Luskentyre Sands has turquoise waters and white fine sands to rival any Polynesian atoll. It's perfect in summer but totally stunning at any time of the year. Plus, it never gets that busy here, even in peak season.

Enjoy a dram
Stop off at nearby Tarbert, Harris's ferry port, where you'll also find the Isle of Harris Distillery. Enjoy a tour and tasting session. And then take a bottle of whisky or gin home to enjoy later (especially for the driver!). We'll leave you to guess which one of us always pulls the designated driver short straw!

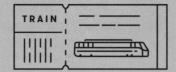

1.
Tenby

Visit one of the most beautiful (and colourful) towns in Wales. This walled wonder is easily one of the best places in Pembrokeshire for a seaside holiday. It's also home to some of the best ice cream in Britain, so be sure to save some stomach space.

Car-free Capers

Top spots you can reach by rail

One of the best parts of travelling around Great Britain is how well connected it is. The UK has one of the best train networks in the world, making it easy to explore the island's nooks and crannies, even if you don't drive. Plus, it's a much greener way to get around, keeping your carbon emissions down, and because you can enjoy a drink while you travel, you can get your holiday started sooner. To feel even more smug, we recommend booking train tickets in advance – you can save a whole heap off your fare this way.

So grab a snack from the trolley, soak up the scenery and read on for some of the best rail-worthy destinations to get you on the right track.

7.
Rye

This East Sussex jewel comes complete with cobbled streets, half-timbered houses and centuries-old pubs. It's been the inspiration for some great works of British literature and Enid Blyton's *The Famous Five: Five go to Smuggler's Top.*

2.
The Cairngorms

Head up north for a healthy dose of adrenaline-fuelled fun, incredible wildlife and perhaps a chance to light a fire in your belly with those strong Scottish whiskies (*see* p. 154 for more on the region ☞).

3.
Windermere

There's nowhere better to experience the water, mountains and scenic overload that is the Lake District – this popular spot makes a great base to explore the national park. When you're here, though, by no means stick to Windermere alone. Catch a bus to Ambleside, Coniston, Grasmere or Keswick.

4.
Brighton

For a little bit of seaside fun! We're talking fun fairground rides, a fantastic beach, a beautiful promenade and some of the best fish and chips in all the land. It's a notoriously lively city, both by the sea and in the centre itself. You can be here in just an hour from London.

5.
St Ives

The quintessential Cornish seaside vacation spot and the perfect place to slow down, kick back and relax!

6.
London
(or another city of your choice!)

British cities are really well connected by rail, with stations usually situated right in the thick of it, making them all pretty easy to visit. Whether you're heading for the bright lights of London or picking someplace less touristy, travelling by train makes perfect sense.

8.
Whitby

See the place where some parts of *Bram Stoker's Dracula* were set. This harbour town (*see* p. 132 ☞) on the Yorkshire coast is also a pretty great spot for fish and chips and general seaside delightfulness.

9.
Eastbourne

Ranked as one of the sunniest places in Britain, Eastbourne is perfect for soaking up some serious seaside vibes. Be sure to pop over to the pier for an afternoon of arcade fun and also to Eastbourne Redoubt – a historic fortress built to defend Britain from Napoleon's army.

Past Treasures

Historical havens to take you back in time

From the grand to the gruesome, there's a slice of British history to suit all curiosities! Harkening back thousands of years, our island is chock-full of transcripts, turrets and intriguing tales.

That being said, it's quite easy to think of Great British history as just towering castles, knights in shining armour and blinged-up royals, right? But trust us, there's all this and lots more to surprise and delight from the different periods that have shaped this island.

If you think historical sites are all hyped-up tourist traps or, worse still, a big snooze-fest – think again. With sealed off plague-ridden villages, smugglers' haunts and mysterious Neolithic sites, our island's history is far from boring.

The spots on this list make excellent daytrip escapes back in time or worthy stop-offs on longer road trips. Either way, you're sure to find a few local treasures.

A past plagued by death

📍 EYAM, ENGLAND

When the Black Death swept Europe in the 1600s, the tiny Peak District village of Eyam became a hotbed of infections. The breakout occurred after a local tailor received some flea-infested cloth from London, and the plague soon spread. To prevent the disease impacting surrounding communities, the villagers agreed to cut themselves off from the rest of the world for over a year! Yeah, we've all had experiences of lockdowns and self-isolation with the Covid-19 pandemic, but this was on another level. Boundary stones (which can still be seen today) were placed around the village to stop people entering or leaving beyond these points. Discover the full story as you wander this historic village, explore the museum and visit Mompesson's Well, where money was exchanged for food from outsiders.

Aristocratic afternoon
After you've explored Eyam, see how the other half lived. Make the 15-minute drive to nearby Chatsworth – the country estate of the Cavendish family since 1549 – and explore the palatial house and gardens.

A popular smugglers' haunt

📍 ROBIN HOOD'S BAY, ENGLAND

Nestled on the North Yorkshire coastline, Robin Hood's Bay is a quaint fishing village and 18th-century smuggling hub. It's made up of tiny cobbled streets and stone alleys that criss-cross a sandy cove. The underground maze of tunnels and passageways allowed smugglers to import contraband items to Britain from France and the Netherlands.

It's obvious that many of the locals had a penchant for liquor and, evidently, not much has changed with the excellent choice of watering holes on offer, like Ye Dolphin with its cosy fire, traditional pub vibes and regional ales. Hankering for a bite? Stop by Tea, Toast and Post, a converted post office cafe that conjures up the best soups in the North East. They host intimate live music evenings, too.

Magnificent Magna Carta

📍 **SALISBURY CATHEDRAL, ENGLAND**

One of our favourite Gothic spots to explore, Salisbury Cathedral is a sacred stunner that's stood here for almost 500 years (and it has the tallest church spire in all the land!). It also houses one of the world's oldest working clocks and the best surviving copy of Magna Carta. This royal charter was agreed between King John of England and his barons in 1215. It cemented certain rights in law, most notably the right to justice and a fair trial. To this day, it's still seen as one of the key building blocks for democracy in Great Britain. While you can't take photos of Magna Carta, you can still get up close to have a good ol' gawk.

A Gothic horror hotspot

📍 **WHITBY ABBEY, ENGLAND**

Just up the road from Robin Hood's Bay on the north-east coast is one of England's most famous and scenic ruins – Whitby Abbey, with over 1500 years of history. Remains of the Benedictine abbey's 13th-century church dominate the headland with eerie foreboding. Once you catch a glimpse, you won't be surprised to learn that the setting inspired Bram Stoker's *Dracula* – the abbey ruins and nearby St Mary's Church even feature in the story. And it's not hard to see why. There's something very mysterious about meandering around the relic on a brisk autumn evening.

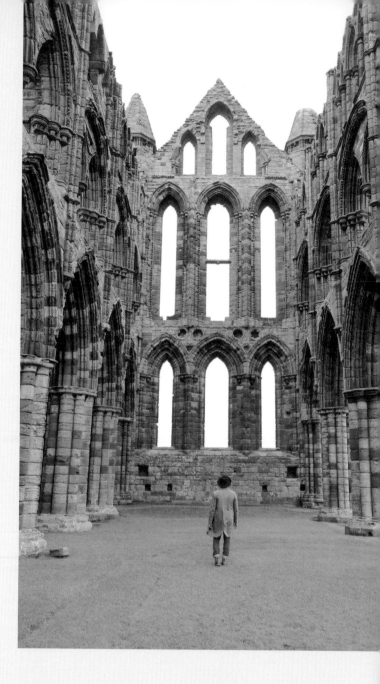

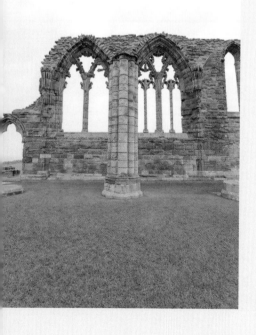

Supper by the sea
Pop down to the historic harbour and pick up some freshly caught fish with chips from the Magpie Cafe. With lashings of vinegar, naturally!

A spectacle made from stone

⚲ STONEHENGE, ENGLAND

Stonehenge needs little introduction – it's one of the most well-known prehistoric sites in the world, believed to have been built around 2500 BCE. There are a number of theories about its purpose: for worship? Healing? An astronomical calendar? Burials? Or a place for a good chinwag?

Speculate at your leisure as you wander around the outside of the stone circle and explore the nearby visitor centre – home to replica Neolithic houses and 250 archaeological objects discovered at the site. The least busy time to visit is the afternoon (check english-heritage.org.uk for up-to-date closing times). Although you can rock up and buy tickets, it's easier to grab them online before you arrive. Tickets have a fixed entry time to limit the number of visitors on site at any time.

Step inside the circle
For a totally special trip, book a 'Stone Circle Experience Ticket' which unlike general admission allows you to enter the stone circle outside of normal opening hours. Be sure to book in advance to get up close to this prehistoric spectacle.

Conquer the castle

📍 CORFE CASTLE, ENGLAND

Perched within Dorset's Purbeck Hills, Corfe Castle has a long and tumultuous history. It was built by William the Conqueror in the 11th century when stone castles became all the rage in Britain. Corfe is a ruin, but there's lots to see – including the terrifying 'murder holes' used to pour boiling liquid and rocks onto any would-be attackers, not to mention wonderful vistas across Purbeck.

Take the train

Make your way to Corfe Castle from nearby Swanage onboard a historic steam train. Or book an 11-mile (18-kilometre) round trip to drive and fire the train yourself (see swanagerailway. co.uk for more information).

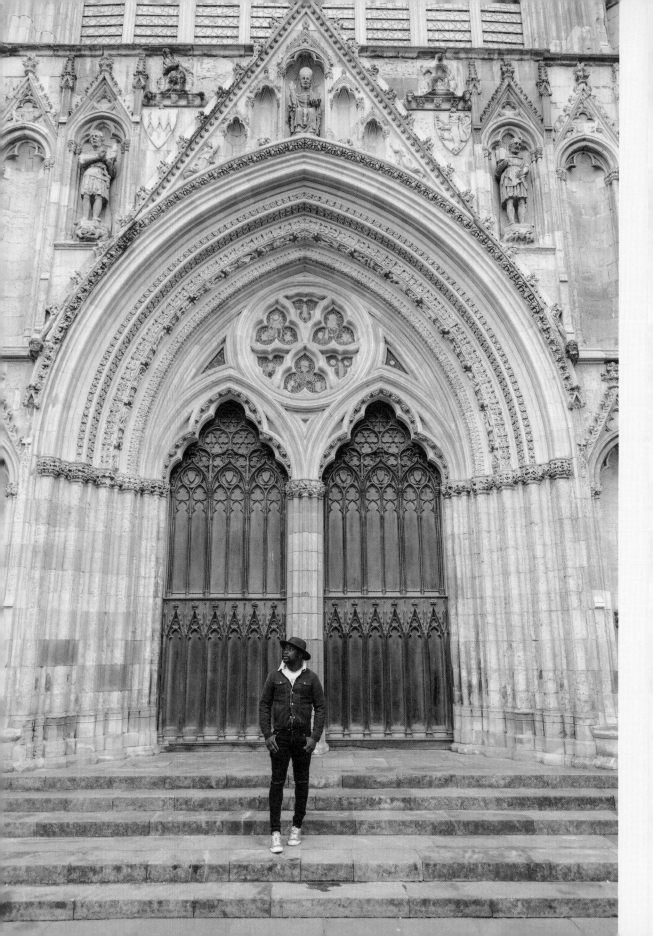

Raise a glass where Guy Fawkes was born

♀ YORK, ENGLAND

You know the 'Guy' we're talking about, right? The man who tried, unsuccessfully, to blow up the Houses of Parliament during the Gunpowder Plot of 1605. He's the bloke we have to thank for Bonfire Night. Well, before his rebellious streak kicked in, he lived in York and was born in what is now the Guy Fawkes Inn. Have a toast in his historic home. Grab yourself a local stout and a scrummy Sunday roast with all the trimmings. York Minster – one of the world's most impressive cathedrals – is just across the road.

↑ The cobbled streets of The Shambles in York

Tread carefully
Avoid stepping on the 'PH' monogram made from cobblestones on North Street – the spot where Protestant Reformer Patrick Hamilton was burned at the stake for his religious beliefs in 1528. Superstitious students (like we were) refuse to walk over the monogram for fear of being cursed. Don't fret though: you can always swim in the North Sea at 5am during the annual May dip to remove the curse. A word of warning … it's teeth-chatteringly cold.

A hole-in-one holiday

♥ ST ANDREWS, SCOTLAND

On Fife's pristine coastline sits the historic town of St Andrews. Despite centuries of history, including its importance as a place of pilgrimage for Christians, it might be best known as the birthplace of golf. The Old Course – the oldest golf course in the world – dates back to the 1700s. It's the perfect place to nail a hole in one! To play a round here, you'll need a certificate showing your current handicap index – the maximum allowed is 36. But St Andrews isn't just about the golf. Wander through the secret tunnels of St Andrews Castle, explore the ruins of the historic abbey and relax on West Sands Beach (see p. 115 ☞).

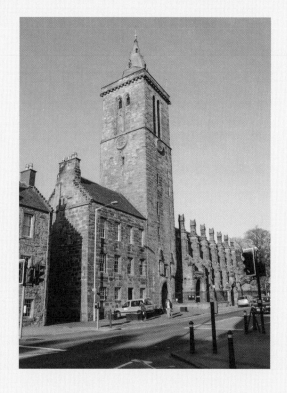

A Neolithic dolmen with connections to Stonehenge

An ancient Welsh marvel

📍 **PENTRE IFAN, WALES**

The largest and best-preserved Neolithic dolmen (a megalithic tomb) in all of Wales, Pentre Ifan is pretty eye-popping to see. Built around 5000 years ago, give or take a few, this ancient burial chamber would originally have been covered with an earthen mound. The stone skeletal remains are all that's left. The Preseli Hills offer a striking backdrop as you explore the site (it's thought that the bluestones at Stonehenge were taken from here and transported all the way to Wiltshire). There's no need to pay or prebook to visit Pentre Ifan, making it a great last-minute stop-off if you're in the area.

Hang out where Henry VIII grew up
⚲ ELTHAM PALACE, ENGLAND

This former palace nestled in the leafy suburb of Eltham, London, may not be on the scale of big-hitters like Buckingham Palace, Kensington and Hampton Court, but there's lots to look at here. Dating back to before the 'Great Survey' of 1086, Eltham Manor, as it was once known, subsequently fell into royal hands – it's where Henry VIII grew up. What makes this palace so special is its two very distinct parts. First, the striking Art Deco rooms commissioned by Stephen and Virginia Courtauld, who lived there in the 1930s, and then the 1400s Great Hall. The latter survived being bombed in World War II. To this day, you can still see the charred wood marks from the fire and falling bombs.

Ghoulish gallivanting
Visit near Halloween for ghoulish tours that highlight all the sightings and sinister happenings that have happened at Eltham over the centuries!

Experience a world of clans and cabers

📍 **BRAEMAR, SCOTLAND**

Held each year, the Braemar Gathering is probably the most famous Highland games event, celebrating Scottish and Celtic culture; think sports like caber toss, tug o' war and hammer throw, combined with traditional music and dancing. It has been going in its present form since 1832, but there's been a gathering of sorts here for around 900 years. Book a ticket online in advance and then find a killer viewpoint. And you'll be in good company – the games are typically attended by members of the royal family.

Designed by Inigo Jones, it was England's first Classical building

The ultimate swear jar

📍 **QUEEN'S HOUSE, ENGLAND**

When Queen Anne of Denmark accidentally shot her husband King James I's dog during a hunt, he was furious and used some pretty offensive language. To apologise for his outburst, the king gifted Anne a new property, which, when it was eventually finished in 1629, became Queen's House in Greenwich. Designed by Inigo Jones, it was England's first Classical building. Today, it's part of Royal Museums Greenwich and home to an impressive art collection. Admire the spiral Tulip Staircase – the first of its kind in England – and the newly designed Great Hall ceiling by Turner Prize winner Richard Wright, which was installed in 2016.

Entry is free. On a lazy day, we love to just chill on the benches inside and soak up this stunner of a house. After you're done, get a bite to eat from nearby Greenwich Market (we love the fluffy doughnuts).

Rise up in Wales's ancient capital

📍 MACHYNLLETH, WALES

After the fierce battles for independence during the Welsh Revolt of 1400, Wales's leader, Owain Glyndŵr, set up the Welsh Parliament in Machynlleth and was crowned Prince of Wales. To this day, you can still see the historic parliament building that sits proudly on the main street (Heol Maengwyn) and learn more about the fascinating facts around the rebellion. After a good gander, head further west through the Dyfi Valley to the Dyfi Osprey Project (a 5-minute drive). Here, you can climb the birdwatching tower and take a peek at the ospreys that call this area home.

From ancient to modern
The town is also home to MOMA Machynlleth, a modern art museum alongside former Wesleyan chapel The Tabernacle. The permeant Tabernacle Collection showcases artists who have lived or worked in Wales.

A real page-turner

Just across the border with England, Hay-on-Wye, known as the 'Town of Books', is a bibliophile's dream spot. Although the town has centuries of history, its biggest draw is the annual Hay Festival of Literature and Arts. Featuring hundreds of award-winning writers and performers celebrating the best of books, it's become a magnet for every bookworm. Former US president Bill Clinton fondly described the festival as 'the Woodstock of the mind'.

Whenever you visit, there are plenty of brilliant booksellers (like the Hay Cinema Bookshop) to work your way through. And every Thursday you can buy treats and treasures from the 700-year-old Hay Market Day (every Thursday 8am till mid-afternoon).

Look at locks of Winston Churchill's hair

📍 **BLENHEIM PALACE, ENGLAND**

Blenheim is the only English palace that isn't owned by the royal family or a bishop's official residence. Built in the 1700s on land gifted to John Churchill, 1st Duke of Marlborough, for his military prowess, it's still one of the largest country houses in all of England and has the regal feels you'd expect from a royal residence. It was also the family home of former prime minister Winston Churchill. After having a good nosey around the rooms and magnificent halls, be sure to spot a golden lock of baby Winston's hair framed on the wall of the room where he was born.

Be a-mazed
Don't forget to explore the estate's Pleasure Gardens and Marlborough Maze. No guarantees you'll get out quickly, though! It's huge – we were totally lost for almost an hour.

Knock it out of the Park

Protected green spaces
to blow your socks off

↑ Sunset reflections in Ullswater, the Lake District

↑ The jagged cliffs of the Pembrokeshire coast

Our island nation is nerdy for national parks. The first was established in 1951, and 70 years later these protected oases are still there for everyone to enjoy free of charge. They take up around 20 per cent of Wales, 11 per cent of England and 9 per cent of Scotland. In total that's 8468 square miles (21,932 square kilometres) of rolling hills, mighty mounts, sandy sanctuaries and watery wonders. Plus, with less than 1 per cent of the total population living within them, these vast rural expanses offer the peace and quiet to immerse yourself in nature.

And they're pretty diverse, too, considering Britain's relatively small size. From the ancient lochs of Scotland and evergreen forests of England to the coastal crooks of Wales, there's something to whet every rural appetite.

When venturing into the Great British wilderness, come prepared – wear suitable clothing, bring snacks and water, and pack a map to find your way (phone signal isn't guaranteed). Visit nationalparks.uk for information about parking, camping and the Countryside Code (the rules for staying safe and protecting the landscapes you're visiting). You can also find out which locations are best for those with access challenges, with 204 more suitable routes around the country to pick from.

There are 15 parks in total – and they're all worth a visit – but we've narrowed them down to our top ten (in no particular order) to make your decision a little easier ᐟᐠ

Peak your interest

📍 **PEAK DISTRICT NATIONAL PARK, ENGLAND**

Britain's first national park, the Peak District encompasses colossal valleys and gorges spanning its length. Once here, you must explore the stunning trails around Winnats Pass (*see* p. 96 ☞) and keep an eye out for the Derby hawkweed (if you're into your flora), as it's the only place in the whole world where it survives.

For an underground experience to remember, visit some of the vast caverns just shy of the national park limit at Poole's Cavern or the Great Masson and Rutland Caverns. Or come back to the surface to cycle the South Peak Loop, taking in 70 miles (112 kilometres) of bridleways, trails and country lanes.

We recommend Edale for a countryside escape (*see* p. 168 ☞), but there are a heap of hillside retreats, cosy cottages and gorgeous glamping spots all over the park.

Go vintage

Why not spend a day touring around in a vintage car? We were chauffeured around in a Model A Ford by vintageadventuretours.co.uk. It was totally cosy sitting back, wrapped up in woollen throws with hot water bottles while we spluttered across the beautiful landscape and learned all about the history of the area.

Sprawling seashore and ancient trees

📍 **SOUTH DOWNS NATIONAL PARK, ENGLAND**

The expansive South Downs is just two hours from London – making it accessible if you live in the capital or perfect to pair with a trip to the big city. At the western fringes you'll find a wonderful walk on the South Downs Way (**see p. 13** ☞) from Cuckmere Haven to Beachy Head, with views across the Seven Sisters cliffs (**see p. 101** ☞). Just be sure to ramble responsibly as those cliff edges are high up and quite unstable.

Heading away from the coast, pop into Petworth House – a glorious 17th-century mansion situated among 700 acres (3 square kilometres) of parkland. Walk the trails and watch out for free-roaming deer.

If you're after forest walks, check out Kingley Vale, just north of Chichester, with winding footpaths and trails that meander past ancient yew trees. It's said to be one of the finest in all of Europe.

Dramatic glacial valleys and lush green hills await you!

Take on the mighty mountain

📍 SNOWDONIA NATIONAL PARK, WALES

Stretching from the Dyfi Valley to the northern coast near Conwy, Snowdonia is the largest and highest national park in Wales. One of the best things to do in Snowdonia is to scale Mt Snowdon itself (*see* p. 152 ☞). There are around six different routes to hike (or take the mountain train), and the views from the top are exceptional.

It's not just Snowdon that makes the region so special. Elsewhere you'll find the historic Talyllyn Railway that runs between Nant Gwernol Station not far from Tal-y-Llyn Lake (Llyn Mwyngil in Welsh) and the town of Tywyn. Here, you can pick up some local ice cream before heading back into Snowdonia.

Just make sure you give yourself plenty of time for pit-stops while exploring the park. You'll be pulling over every five minutes to marvel at glacial valleys and rugged alpine tundra. Mae'n bert iawn! (It's very pretty!)

A slice of Italy
After exploring the national park, head to the village of Portmeirion (*see* p. 59 ☞) a few hundred metres from the border of the park (near the town of Porthmadog). With its distinct Mediterranean vibe, you'll feel like you've been transported to the Amalfi Coast.

Ancient woodlands and medieval marvels

📍 **EXMOOR NATIONAL PARK, ENGLAND**

Perched almost halfway between St Ives (in Cornwall) and Bristol, Exmoor National Park is the perfect place to visit for a few days in the great outdoors.

Within the greater Exmoor area, you'll find over 2500 hectares (6180 acres) of ancient semi-natural woodlands (those that have developed naturally but have been managed by humans). On the coastline, just west of Lynton, is the Valley of Rocks – a dry U-shaped valley made up of striking prehistoric rock formations. Wringcliff Bay, in particular, is truly gorgeous. If you're further inland, walk the trails over the medieval Tarr Steps bridge.

Adrenaline seekers should head towards the northern coastline for a spot of cliff jumping, coasteering and kayaking with Exmoor Adventures (exmooradventures.co.uk).

Here's an i-deer
Red deer have called Exmoor home since prehistoric times. On a clear day, you can see herds of them roaming the hills, and if you visit in July, you might even spot some calves. Increase your chances on a deer safari. We headed out with the legends at Red Stag Safari (redstagsafari.co.uk).

↑ The medieval Tarr Steps – an ancient clapper bridge in Exmoor

The jewel in Scotland's crown

♀ CAIRNGORMS NATIONAL PARK, SCOTLAND

Named for the mountain range that forms part of the park, this Scottish behemoth covers over 1700 square miles (4500 square kilometres), and there's lots to see – so it's well worth a couple of trips. One of the first places most people visit (especially when travelling from Inverness) is Aviemore, a gateway to the great outdoors beyond (*see* p. 183 ☞).

For a more secluded spot, get on yer (mountain) bike or rent one from a local hire centre and head over to Loch an Eilein. It's eerily quiet and the ruined castle on an island in the centre is stunning. While you've got your bike to hand, ride the woodland trail to An Lochan Uaine – The Green Lochan (a lochan is a small loch).

Legend has it that the water's vibrant green colour is caused by the king of the fairies, who uses it to wash his clothes!

The Cairngorms is home to one of Queen Elizabeth's favourite places: Balmoral Castle. From Aberdeen, the estate is a 70-minute drive. You can have a guided tour and feel truly regal! Afterwards, take a hike to the Cairns of Balmoral – stone pyramids, many of which were built during Queen Victoria's reign to commemorate life events of members of the royal family. Ask for directions at the local tourist information centre at Crathie and make sure you bring a map (or offline navigations) as sometimes the routes are hard to spot.

Drive time
If you want to explore most of the park by car, follow the Snow Roads Scenic Route that stretches from Blairgowrie to Grantown-on-Spey. It's a great drive to take in the park's small villages, distilleries and glacial landscapes.

Up hill and down dale

📍 **YORKSHIRE DALES NATIONAL PARK, ENGLAND**

The Yorkshire Dales National Park is one of Northern England's most protected areas, and it's easy to see why. One of our favourite spots is Hardraw Force Waterfall near Hawes – England's largest, single-drop waterfall. The walk to the falls itself is relatively easy, though a bit muddy in wetter weather, but that shouldn't dampen your experience. It has a reported 100-foot (30-metre) drop, and the views from above and below are spectacular.

Another natural site not to be missed, about 30 minutes' drive from the market town of Skipton, is Malham Cove, a colossal curved cliff that was carved out over thousands of years by glacial melt (**see p. 99** ☞). The climb to the top is steep, so be prepared for that and wear some sturdy shoes!

Go underground

Take a trip to Gaping Gill, a large shaft and cave with a massive waterfall flowing inside. You can arrange to get winched down into the cave itself. Check cravenpotholeclub.org for updates and, weather permitting, winch events. Pack some waterproofs and make the 90-minute walk from Clapham. On the way you'll pass Ingleborough Cave, which is well worth a gander, too.

A watery wonderland

📍 **LAKE DISTRICT NATIONAL PARK, ENGLAND**

The Lake District might just be our favourite national park in England. From strolling through Ambleside, paddleboarding on Ullswater and hiking Helm Crag to trying your hand at sailing on Windermere, if it's action you're after, the Lake District won't disappoint. The park has plenty of cosy getaways and sumptuous hotel spots along its many lake shores for those looking for a more sedate stay.

And for literary fans, Beatrix Potter is a big deal in the region. The Lake District inspired some of her most famous children's books, and later in life she worked closely with the National Trust, helping it to acquire land and preserve the scenery she loved. Visit Hill Top, her home in Near Sawrey, or the 19th-century Wray Castle near Ambleside, a favourite holiday spot when she was a kid.

Coastal vistas and animal magic

📍 PEMBROKESHIRE COAST NATIONAL PARK, WALES

On the westerly shores of South Wales, Pembrokeshire Coast is the only national park centred on the shoreline.

Be sure to explore Carew Castle, a historic ruin 20 minutes from the sea – it's so beautiful at sunset (from Mill Pond). Also, head along the coastal path to see the Green Bridge (**see p. 102** ☞), a natural limestone arch, and explore some of the many other scheduled ancient monuments (nationally important archaeological sites).

Along your travels, you'll easily spot pods of dolphins, puffins (June–July), gannets and seals, who love the area as much as we do. As the Welsh would say, it's lush!

In the more northerly limits is Newport. Not to be confused with the city of Newport in South East Wales, Newport in Pembrokeshire is a tiny town filled with local eateries, watering holes and antique stores – perfect for an afternoon stroll.

~~~~~~~~~~~~~~~~~~~~~~~

Say farewell to Dobby

If you love the beach (and are a bit of a Harry Potter fan), take a trip to Freshwater West. Not only is it a sandy paradise for a good old splash around, it's also a filming location used for *Harry Potter and the Deathly Hallows: Part 1* and *Part 2* (where Shell Cottage was located) and Dobby's final resting place.

~~~~~~~~~~~~~~~~~~~~~~~

Bonnie banks and gorgeous glens

📍 **LOCH LOMOND AND THE TROSSACHS NATIONAL PARK, SCOTLAND**

Consisting of an abundance of lochs, glens and dramatic mountains, Loch Lomond and The Trossachs is just north of Glasgow. You can't visit here without stopping off at Loch Lomond, especially as it's the largest inland stretch of water in Britain. Just off the A82, which runs the length of the loch, be sure to stop off at Inveruglas to look out from An Ceann Mòr – an unusual pyramid-shaped viewpoint – before hopping on a boat to cruise the loch itself.

To the east near Aberfoyle you'll find Loch Ard. Although smaller than Loch Lomond, it's just as beautiful. And stop for fantastic views over Loch Restil at the fondly named Rest and Be Thankful Viewpoint (just off the A83) between the towering Beinn an Lochain and Beinn Ime.

Starry skies and Roman heritage

📍 **NORTHUMBERLAND NATIONAL PARK, ENGLAND**

Hugging the border between England and Scotland, Northumberland National Park is home to part of Hadrian's Wall. Stretching all the way from the North Sea to the Irish Sea, this fortification was built in 122 CE to guard the Roman Empire's northern frontier. Along the wall, explore the Temple of Mithras (dedicated to the god Roman soldiers adored), Vindolanda (a vast ruined fort) and Housesteads Roman Fort, where you can see remains of the barracks, hospital and some pretty old toilets. The latter is more interesting than it sounds!

For night owls, Northumberland National Park is great for stargazing. It contains an International Dark Sky Park – one of the biggest areas of protected night sky in all of Europe. You can even spot the Andromeda Galaxy with your naked eyes! Just keep your fingers crossed for a clear night.

If you really want to stretch your legs, scale the Cheviot, the park's highest peak. Although this is not not an endurance-style hike, you will need a good level of fitness to reach the very tippy-top. From here, on a crisp and clear day, you might even be able to see Edinburgh in the distance.

Go Treasure-hunting

Stores and stalls to shop till you drop

From eclectic markets and gorgeous galleries to prestigious shopping parades, our fair island has a heap of spend-worthy spots to suit every taste and budget. Whether you're looking to splurge like a celeb or hunt down vintage finds and foodie favourites, we've got you covered.

Borough Market
♀ LONDON

Set in Southwark near to London Bridge, this is the city's most famous foodie market, packed with fine purveyors, watering holes and takeaway treats to set your stomach growling. The stalls are relatively seasonal, so what's on offer will depend on when you visit (and it's not open on Sundays). Grab a slab of cheese from the Borough Cheese Company or head to The Gated Garden for every plant under the sun – it's a haven for foliage-friendly shoppers. To keep costs low, visit 30 minutes before closing time when lots of stalls discount produce.

St Nicholas Indoor Market
♀ BRISTOL

This covered market (known locally as St Nicks) in the heart of the city has been going since 1743. Open all week long, it's a treasure trove of gifts, original fashion and hand-crafted accessories. You'll find everything from crystals and antique furniture to fantastic food.

Abergavenny Market
♀ ABERGAVENNY

As popular with the locals as it is with visitors, this is a perfect port of call when exploring the town. The General Market runs on Tuesdays, Fridays and Saturdays, and has everything from vintage finds to veggies. There is also a heap of seasonal and regular events you won't want to miss, like its weekly flea market (Wednesdays) and the monthly craft and antique fairs.

Kirkgate Market
♀ LEEDS

As one of Europe's largest indoor markets, Kirkgate is hard to miss and well worth a visit. Since 1857, it's served the local community with a diverse mix of over 200 stalls, from yummy bakeries to barbers. Pick up groceries and stop by some of the street food vendors as you shop (any day except Sundays). Fat Annie's makes a killer meat-free hotdog and Jenny's Jerk Chicken is just delicious – be sure to try the curried goat.

George Street
♀ EDINBURGH

Perched behind Princes Street's parade of international brands and high-street stores, George Street is in the heart of Edinburgh's elegant New Town. Originally a residential area, it was transformed into a shopping destination by the Victorians. Now with high-end boutiques, bars and foodie spots (we love The Dome and The Grill Room), it's one of the city's best places to splash out on something special.

Regent Street
📍 LONDON

If flagship stores and designer decor are more your scene, head to Regent Street – London's original shopping destination. This Regency-era architectural gem curves to connect Piccadilly Circus with Oxford Street. You'll find luxury labels, places to be pampered and award-winning restaurants along the 'Mile of Style'. While you're in the area, duck into Liberty on Great Marlborough Street – a luxury department store built in the 1920s – or Carnaby Street's independent fashion boutiques.

Scottish Antique and Arts Centre
📍 ABERNYTE

Around a 20-minute drive from Dundee, the Scottish Antique and Arts Centre boasts thousands of collectables, antiques and stylish homewares that are too good to miss. Once inside, you'll find a heap of dealers that all specialise in something unique, like Antique Prints of Scotland, which sells lovingly restored vintage maps. With free parking and wheelchair access throughout, it's a great stop off on a Scottish road trip.

Norwich Market
📍 NORWICH

Easily one of the largest and oldest open-air markets in Great Britain, Norwich Market is steeped in history and has an eclectic mix of stalls to explore – from vintage clothes and haberdashery to pet supplies, plants and video games. You're sure to work up an appetite browsing the nearly 200 stalls on offer – luckily there are plenty of options for foodies, too. Just don't visit on a Sunday, when most stalls are closed.

Hay-on-Wye
📍 WALES

Fondly known as the 'town of books' and home to the world-renowned Hay Festival (see p. 145 ☞), this Welsh wonder, just over the border with England, is home to around 20 independent bookshops, including ones that specialise in maps, natural history and children's literature. Offering everything from rare finds to modern classics, it's a must-visit shopping spree spot for any bookworm. We love Richard Booth's Bookshop – a bookstore, cinema and event space with a tasty cafe.

The Lanes
📍 BRIGHTON

A trip to Brighton isn't complete without a leisurely stroll around The Lanes – a mix of tightly packed streets and twisting alleys that make up Brighton's historic quarter. Here, you'll find a host of galleries, boutique fashion shops and some of the city's best bars and restaurants. You can easily spend a morning here and finish off your day at the Royal Pavilion or follow the fairground squeals and smell of candy floss to Brighton Pier! Just bring us back a stick of rock.

Baltic Triangle,
📍 LIVERPOOL

This historically industrial area has blossomed into a thriving creative quarter filled with indie start-ups, studio spaces and eclectic shops and eateries. There's always something going on – from vintage markets to pop-up restaurants – making it the perfect area to stroll and soak up the street art. Spend hours rummaging through Red Brick Vintage – a wonderful warehouse of vintage clothing and bric-a-brac inside an old brewery – then stop by the Baltic Social for their punk afternoon tea and boss music.

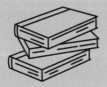

Escape to the Country

Rural idylls ripe
for recharging

Escaping to the countryside is a pursuit that's best served relaxed! Regardless of where you call home, a little getaway into the great outdoors and a stay at a cosy countryside retreat can be an enriching experience for any type of traveller. Whether you're looking for log-fire cabins, coastal hideouts, quaint villages or chocolate-box market towns, Britain has them all in spades.

Here we've picked our favourite off-grid getaways for those wanting something rustic and serene. But while adventuring to the middle of nowhere is fun, it can be a bit of a pain driving down country lanes for hours for a quick weekend break. So, in the spirit of more eco-friendly travel and accessibility, we've included some spots that are close to public transport hubs.

Shake off any ideas of muddy puddles, strenuous hikes and stale cheese rolls, and relish some of the best countryside capers Britain has to offer. 👍

Watergate Bay
♀ ENGLAND

Just shy of Newquay in Cornwall, Watergate Bay is a coastal retreat that ticks all the boxes. The bay itself is totally glorious and the golden sandy beach is just too good to miss on a warm summer's day.

Not only that, it's a pretty epic spot to perfect your surfing skills. If you're a total novice (like us), you can hire surfboards, organise lessons with the pros and master those waves. Though, as complete amateurs, we were totally shattered after about 30 minutes and headed to dry land for some sticky toffee pudding. We always have our minds on pudding, and the nearby Watergate Bay Hotel is a great spot for some hearty, freshly baked treats. Just shy of Cornwall Airport Newquay or the nearby train station, it's easy to visit if you don't drive.

Walk it off
Include Watergate Bay as part of a wider trip around the South West Coast Path (*see p. 10* ☞) or use the bay as your base to stroll to the Carnewas at Bedruthan towering sea stacks.

Malton
⚲ ENGLAND

On the edge of the Howardian Hills Area of Outstanding Natural Beauty (AONB, an area protected by law to conserve and enhance its existing loveliness) lies Malton. The Yorkshire market town might be small, but it has more than enough captivating countryside and award-winning food to sate any appetite.

After arriving (with tummies rumbling, of course), be sure to take your time wandering around the central marketplace. You'll find independent storefronts stocked with local suppliers, serving up some of the best treats in all of Yorkshire. From bakers and butchers to artisanal coffee roasters and micro-brewers, you'll be spoilt for choice. Check out patisserie spot Florian Poirot for melt-in-your-mouth macarons, The Groovy Moo for yummy gelato and Stew & Oyster Malton for sumptuous puds.

Food, glorious food!
If you want more than just the shops, plan your trip alongside Malton's food market that's typically held every second Saturday of the month – it's arguably one of Yorkshire's most-renowned and delicious stomach-stuffing pilgrimages.

Edale

⦿ ENGLAND

Nestled in the heart of the Peak District National Park (but with its own train station for easy access), Edale is a tiny village that feels a million miles away from everyday life. Historically, the village comprised a collection of herdsman shelters. Nowadays, there's a quaint pub and a few independent cafes to grab a bite. It's at the trailhead for the Pennine Way (see p. 13 ☞), one of Great Britain's celebrated long-distance walking paths, and a 10-minute drive to limestone gorge Winnats Pass (see p. 96 ☞).

Stay in a cosy lodge tent at Edale Gathering (edalegathering.com), equipped with roaring fire burner, heated bed and all the mod-cons. It's enchanting, regardless of what time of year you visit.

Billingshurst

📍 ENGLAND

Squirreled away between the Surrey Hills (AONB), South Downs National Park (see p. 151 ☞) and High Weald (AONB), Billingshurst provides ample opportunities for a countryside escape. There are lush rolling hills, tranquil canal trails – we walked the 8-mile (13-kilometre) Wey and Arun Canal circular – and nearby Petworth House, inspired by the Baroque palaces of Europe. Or why not turn your trip into a wine-tasting tour? This region has a similar chalky soil to Champagne in France. It's the perfect place to visit a vineyard and try some English sparkling wine – Nyetimber and Tinwood Estate (see p. 58 ☞) are two of our favourites. Book tours, tastings and lodgings in advance.

You'll find lots of independently run accommodation options in the area. We stayed in The Haven in an Airship (a glass and aluminium pod) hidden among the trees, with a roaring fire, gorgeous views and cosy nooks. It was bliss, and only 90 minutes from London.

Lacock

📍 **ENGLAND**

Huddled within the rolling hills of
Wiltshire – a 10-minute taxi ride from
Chippenham train station – Lacock has
barely changed over the last 200 years.
The vast majority of the village is owned
by the National Trust, which has taken
stewardship of its conservation and
stunning stone cottages.

While you're snapping away, you
might be interested to learn that Lacock
was home to William Henry Fox Talbot,
a polymath and pioneer of Victorian
photography. His house, the 13th-century
Lacock Abbey, was where the first photos
on paper were created in 1839. You can
take a leisurely gander around his old
haunt, explore the Fox Talbot Museum and
scoff some scones at the local tearoom.

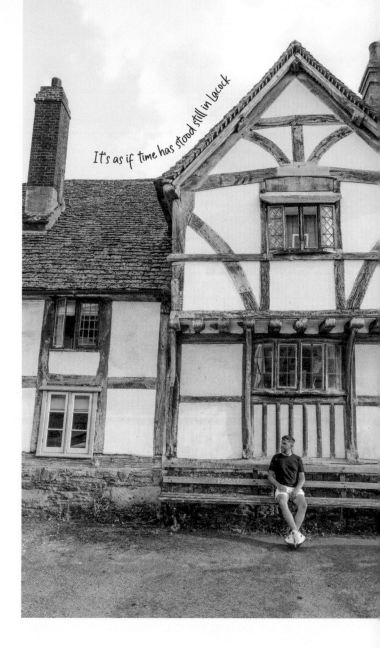

It's as if time has stood still in Lacock

For cottage lovers
Stay a little longer by booking a couple
of nights at 2 High Street, a National
Trust cottage. Think thick wooden beams,
horse-hair walls and snuggly little rooms.

Craster

📍 **ENGLAND**

Perched overlooking the choppy North Sea, Craster on the Northumberland coast is a centuries-old fishing village where it feels as if time has stood still. The nearest train station is Alnmouth, 20 minutes' drive away – we rented a car from near Morpeth or you can organise a taxi pick-up. After spending some time wandering the shorefront, be sure to explore the ruins of the 14th-century Dunstanburgh Castle. And don't leave without trying the famous Craster Kippers.

Hartland Peninsular

♀ ENGLAND

Heading west from Barnstaple, Devon, you'll find a truly peaceful and wildly beautiful stretch of coast. The Hartland Peninsular is an AONB. Once here, be sure to stop in the tiny fishing village of Clovelly, which is filled with higgledy-piggledy stone cottages and has a picturesque harbour. Or wander the trails near Speke's Mill Mouth Waterfall and Hartland Abbey. There are lots of unique places to stay around the Hartland Peninsular. We booked into Loveland Farm (loveland.farm) – with its massive eco-friendly pods to watch the starry skies, super-comfy beds and an indoor swimming pool, it's a stunning place to stay.

Possibly one of England's quaintest little towns ...

Rye and Camber Sands

📍 ENGLAND

Just shy of High Weald AONB, Rye is an ancient little town with cobbled streets (we loved Mermaid Street), charity shops and antique spots galore (we loved The Quay Antiques and Collectables), especially around the Strand. A hop, skip and a 10-minute drive away is Camber Sands. Look out over the English Channel and chill out on the dunes. The perfect countryside/coastal combo. If you're driving, why not stop off at stunning Bodiam Castle (*see* p. 26 ☞) or head onto the water at River Rother for some paddleboarding or kayaking.

Smuggle a few pints

Make a pit-stop at Rye's Mermaid Inn – a hotel, pub and restaurant with cellars dating back to the 1100s. This was the watering hole à la mode for local smuggling outfit the Hawkhurst Gang back in the 1700s. It's even said that their ghosts haunt the building. Spooky!

Ullswater

📍 ENGLAND

Ullswater is one of the Lake District's 16 tranquil bodies of water. The whole national park is epic (*see p. 157* ☞), but if you're hankering for a really restful and undisturbed stay, this is the spot.

It stretches from Pooley Bridge to Glenridding and nearby Patterdale, and the sights are best appreciated from aboard the Ullswater Steamer, historic vessels you can hop on and off at various points, or you could try paddleboarding for a more active outing.

If you're a walker, the hike up to Place Fell can be completed in a morning. Oh, and stop off at Aira Force Waterfall and take to the trails up to Hallin Fell (*see p. 10* ☞).

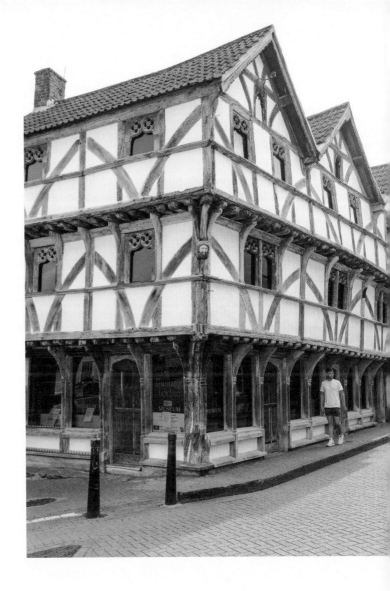

Axbridge

♀ **ENGLAND**

On the fringe of the Mendip Hills AONB, Axbridge offers a countryside retreat without compromising on tasty restaurants, vintage shops and independent pubs. Stay in the historic town centre, where you'll find Tudor gem King John's Hunting Lodge – a former wool merchant's house and local history museum – and a vibrant square and high street. For even fresher air, take a wander via the Strawberry Line walking route right into the Mendips. Axbridge is a 45-minute walk from Cheddar, where you'll find the famous Cheddar Gorge (see p. 98 ☞), caves and lots of delicious cheese.

Gower Peninsula

📍 **WALES**

Within easy reach of Swansea, the Gower Peninsula might be a stone's throw from the city, but it feels like a million miles away. It's renowned for its stunning coastline and beaches, and you'll be spoiled for choice at Three Cliffs Bay and Oxwich Bay. Enjoy a classic '99' and stroll down the pier at The Mumbles. Then head to Rhossili Bay later in the day to watch the sun set. Those orangey hues are fire at dusk!

Cardigan Bay

⚲ WALES

Stretching the whole westerly groove of Wales's coastline, from Pembrokeshire all the way around to the Llyn Peninsula, Cardigan Bay is a gem to explore. You can spend a good few years coming back to the coastline here and not get bored. One of our favourite spots is Aberaeron, a tiny town that sits right between Cardigan and Aberystwyth. It's got a vibrant and historic harbour where you can buy locally made honey ice cream from The Hive and enjoy tasty food at the award-winning Harbourmaster restaurant (**see p. 107** ☞).

If you're after pristine beaches, stop off at Ynyslas (just shy of Borth), where you'll be greeted with gorgeous dunes and beautiful sunsets. Or try Penbryn Beach (**see p. 58** ☞) and stay at Fforest (coldatnight.co.uk), a retreat that has everything from cosy yurts to a rustic farmhouse. It's a total gem and the perfect place to switch off, spend a few nights and totally unwind.

↑ Cave exploring on Penbryn Beach

Who said to just build sandcastles on the beach?

For the explorer
Take the train to Carmarthen and hire some wheels from the town to drive your way towards Cardigan Bay. Alternatively, take the train that covers the northern part of Cardigan Bay (we'd suggest from Machynlleth) and buy the Explore Cambrian Day ticket, which allows you to hop on and off as you please.

Plockton

♀ SCOTLAND

Plockton is often said to be the 'Jewel of the Highlands', and rightly so! This picture-perfect village overlooks the pristine shores of Loch Carron, affording fabulous views in every direction.

As soon as you arrive, head on down to the historic harbour front and off on one of the boats that traverse the loch. We boarded the *Sula Mhor* with Calum's Seal Trips (calums-sealtrips.com) and loved every second. Along the way you'll spot seals and, if you're lucky, majestic golden eagles that hunt in the area.

While there is a train station at nearby Duncraig, we'd recommend driving here or hiring a car in the area. That way you'll be able to explore all the nearby lochs and even pop over to the Isle of Skye (see p. 39 ☞).

Arisaig

📍 **SCOTLAND**

Found in the Lochaber area of the Highlands, Arisaig is a peaceful, undisturbed village. Over the years, it's been home to Vikings and various notable clans. These days Arisaig is the kind of place you can really slow down and take in the beauty of the region. Join a private foraging course in nearby spots like Moidart. We headed out with Wildwood Bushcraft (wildwoodbushcraft.com), who helped us forage for wild plants and shellfish to rustle up a feast right on the beach. Their expertise means you can forage safely, learn all about 'wild eating' and cooking up your bounty for a unique gastronomic experience.

Aviemore

📍 SCOTLAND

Located in the heart of the Cairngorms National Park (**see p. 154** ☞), Aviemore is a gateway to explore the unspoilt wilderness of this vast natural landscape, spanning over 1700 square miles (4500 square kilometres)! From mountain-biking, rambling and quad-biking to hiking round the park's stunning lochs (and keeping your eyes peeled for deer), it's all about the nature here.

After a day in the great outdoors, enjoy a hearty venison stew or veggie haggis from The Druie Café (just 5 minutes from Aviemore). Then, hotfoot it to the Old Bridge Inn (oldbridgeinn.co.uk) for drinks and live music – don't forget to make a reservation.

Wander on the Wild Side

Locales for
nature-lovers

Britain is home to some amazing wildlife, and we are suckers for it! Maybe it's all the David Attenborough documentaries we watched growing up or just our fierce fascination with spotting animals in the wild ... we're obsessed. And while you won't find lions, tigers or bears in Great Britain, there are so many special species dotted all across our beautiful island.

One positive side effect of the Covid-19 lockdowns was the chance for wildlife to thrive without interference from us pesky humans. From birdsong in cities and sightings of rare species to cheeky foxes getting up to mischief, it gave us the chance to slow down and appreciate the animals all around us.

Make the most of this new-found love for nature on your next getaway. Whether you want the full safari experience or a one-off critter encounter as part of your trip, these fauna-focused destinations have lots to offer.

While you can get pretty close to some of the animals mentioned here, it's worth bringing binoculars or a zoom lens with you when you're out scouting for wildlife, particularly when it comes to skittish animals – and if you need to keep your distance to help protect habitats.

Keep your voice down, your eyes peeled and get ready to discover some of our island's most fascinating residents. ✌

For seal pups, whales and seabirds

📍 **FARNE ISLANDS, ENGLAND**

The Farne Islands National Nature Reserve off the Northumberland coast is a treasure trove of Great British wildlife. From the famous seal residents (and their cute pups) to the dolphins, whales and puffins in the water, it's truly incredible. If you're looking for maximum cuteness, the first seal pups start to arrive in September, so plan your visit accordingly. Birdwatchers will have a field day – many sea birds (guillemots, kittiwakes and razorbills, to mention a few) call this beautiful part of England home. The best way to make the most of it is to hop aboard one of the boat tours leaving from Seahouses.

Lighthouse lovely
Stop off at Longstone Lighthouse on Longstone Rock and discover the fascinating tale of Grace Darling – the lighthouse keeper's daughter who helped rescue crew and passengers from a terrifying shipwreck here in 1838.

For ponies and birds of prey

📍 **EXMOOR NATIONAL PARK, ENGLAND**

There are two four-legged reasons why you might visit Exmoor National Park – the red deer and the enchanting wild ponies. The latter are native to Britain and roam freely on the moors. They're not technically wild, being owned by farmers or the National Trust, but it's a great place to see the species in their natural habitat.

Exmoor also has some incredible birds of prey – kestrels, red kites and peregrines are not uncommon. And don't get us started on the wild grouse! They're everywhere here. Before we went to Exmoor, we'd only ever seen grouse a few times (one in particular terrified us when it jumped out of the bushes during an evening walk on the Isles of Scilly). But in Exmoor, they're all over the place.

Literary location

Exmoor's natural beauty has served as inspiration for a number of famous writers. Before you visit, we recommend reading Lorna Doone by R. D. Blackmore, published in 1869. You'll recognise a lot of real-life locations from the book when you're exploring.

For super salmon

⚲ ROGIE FALLS, SCOTLAND

While Rogie Falls aren't extraordinary on their own merit, once a year, they really come alive. About a 30-minute drive from Inverness, this is one of the best places in Britain to see salmon jump, as they return upstream after years out in the ocean to spawn and complete their life cycle. Watching them try to make the 19-foot (6-metre) leap up the waterfall is truly impressive.

The best time of year to see this awesome spectacle is August and September. Make it part of a trip to the Highlands – the Cairngorms (**see below** 👇) are only an hour away by car.

For really rare sightings

⚲ THE CAIRNGORMS, SCOTLAND

The Cairngorms mountain range in the eastern Scottish Highlands is one of the best areas to visit in Great Britain if you're looking for some outstanding outdoor fun (it's one of the few places in the UK where you can ski on snow, on a real mountain). But if you've come purely for the wildlife, you won't be disappointed. This is the place to see red deer roaming in the wild. Golden eagles, red squirrels, ospreys, ptarmigan and mountain hare are also common. In fact, 25 per cent of Great Britain's threatened species can be found there. For more on the Cairngorms, (*see* p. 154 ☞).

Awesome aurora
It's possible to see the Northern Lights in the Cairngorms. For your best chance, head over to the coastal area up north where there's likely to be less cloud cover, and follow local alerts and Twitter feeds to find out when visibility is most likely.

For deer near the city

You go to Richmond Park in London for the deer – red deer and fallow deer, to be more precise. It's one of the best places in Britain to see them, perhaps in large part because, unlike other deer, they've grown accustomed to people being in close proximity, so they're not as skittish. That means you can take amazing photographs and get a closer look. The park is also a lovely part of London, making it the perfect spot for a picnic, a lazy day out or even a run, if you're so inclined.

Unexpected critters
Keep your eyes peeled for grass snakes – don't worry, they're not venomous. Oh, and if you're lucky, you might spot a rose-ringed parakeet! These brightly coloured characters aren't endemic to the area – the local population is thought to be the result of pet birds being released or making a flight to freedom.

For beavers and their brilliance

📍 **KNAPDALE FOREST, SCOTLAND**

Up in Argyll and Bute, in the Scottish Highlands, you'll find Knapdale, a gorgeous spot that's regarded as Scotland's very own rainforest. While the scenery's fantastic, the real reason to visit is it's one of the few places in Britain where you can see beavers in the wild – they were re-introduced to the area back in 2009 after becoming extinct in the 16th century. And they're absolutely thriving. The profound effect they have on the environment, felling trees and creating dams, which can cause lakes to form, is nothing short of impressive.

Two-wheeled wander
Hop on your bike and explore the forest from two wheels. There are great cycle trails to traverse, taking you through a whole host of different habitats – from woodlands to wetlands.

For a puffin-perfect getaway

📍 **LUNDY ISLAND, ENGLAND**

Lundy Island, off the North Devon coast, is home to a wild variety of species both above and below the waves. It's importance to British wildlife led to it becoming the UK's first Marine Conservation Zone (a special designation to help protect an area's wildlife or natural habitat). Expect to see puffins (the reason lots of people visit the island), sika deer, pygmy shrew, seals and even wild ponies. Lundy is also home to some really rare birds, making it a much-loved spot for birdwatchers. For more on Lundy Island, *see p. 44* ☞.

For red squirrels and wild otters

📍 **KIELDER FOREST, ENGLAND**

Kielder is the largest forest in England and, arguably, one of the most important for British wildlife. It's home to 50 per cent of the English red squirrel population and an impressive number of badgers, roe deer and ospreys. You'll also find water voles and goshawks here (they're particularly hard to see elsewhere in Britain) and the country's only venomous snake – the adder – so make sure you tread lightly! If you go wild for wild otters, head over to Bakethin Nature Reserve (on the northern end of Kielder Water) for a chance to see these cuties.

For the full dolphin experience

📍 CARDIGAN BAY, WALES

Cardigan Bay (*see p. 179* ☞) is hands down one of the best places in Great Britain to see dolphins. We recommend taking a boat trip – make sure you book in advance if you're only here for a short time. Not sure about your sea legs? There's a good chance you'll still spot them from the shore. Our first sighting, back when we lived in Wales, was when we were casually sat at home overlooking the water and one jumped straight up in front of us. And then the others joined in – it was like something out of a nature documentary.

↑ The rainbow houses of Aberaeron

Wondrous Watering Holes

Pubs and bars to wet any whistle

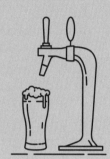

We Brits love a good pub! From cosy local haunts to an underground speakeasy, we have it all. Over the years, we've developed a pretty extensive tipple-tasting repertoire – all in the name of research, naturally! To help you find the finest cocktails, hot toddy or boozy backwater, we've collected a few of our favourites. Now, who's getting the drinks in?

Canal Street
⚲ MANCHESTER

For a fun-fuelled night to remember, head to Canal Street – Manchester's unmissable LGBTQIA+ destination. On the weekend, it's packed with people and so much fun! With over 40 venues all within a short walk of the Rochdale Canal, it's a place to drink, dance and party hard with your mates. Head to G-A-Y Manchester for plenty of iconic hits and good vibes. Just wear comfy shoes – you'll be dancing the night away!

Canal Street, Manchester

Bussey Rooftop Bar
⚲ LONDON

With 360-degree views across London from the top of Peckham's iconic Bussey Building, this is a great place for a summer evening swig while the sun is setting. Surrounded by twinkling lights, grab an Aperol spritz and munch on oven-fired pizza from Share A Slice (ours is the double chorizo, if you're buying). What's more, for every pizza they serve, they'll donate one to people in need.

Bussey Building,
133 Rye Ln, London

Panda & Sons
⚲ EDINBURGH

On the street, Panda & Sons looks like an unassuming barber's – but don't let that fool you. Behind those red doors lies a subterranean delight with a speakeasy vibe and some of the best mixologists in the capital. It's a perfect venue for a date when you want to impress. You'll be in for a total treat with their unique and quirky concoctions. We had the famous Birdcage made with lemongrass and rhubarb. Yum!

79 Queen St, Edinburgh

Bombay Sapphire Distillery
⚲ WHITCHURCH

Tucked away in rural Hampshire, a short drive from Basingstoke, is the picturesque home of Bombay Sapphire gin. Enjoy guided tours around the gorgeous converted mill alongside a tipple (or three). Gin lovers will be in in their element. Something to celebrate? Book a gin masterclass in advance with some of the best mixologists in the business.

Laverstoke Mill,
London Rd, Whitchurch

Peggy's Skylight
♀ NOTTINGHAM

Peggy's Skylight is a live jazz venue that hosts a range of national and international acts and prides itself on its combination of great music and Middle Eastern cuisine. For the best view of the action, request a table in the 'Billie' or 'Mingus' sections. You can easily spend a whole night lounging in the vintage theatre seating and soaking up the 1930s vibes here.

3 George St, Nottingham

Ty Coch Inn
♀ PORTHDINLLAEN

This cosy and totally traditional Welsh watering hole in the historic fishing village of Porthdinllaen is well worth visiting on a sunny afternoon. It's right on the unspoiled Llyn Peninsula shorefront, with gorgeous views across the Irish Sea, making it a great place to chill out with family and friends. Be sure to try some of their local guest ales. And if you're the designated driver, be aware that you'll need to walk a little way to park as the main road is for residents only.

Porthdinllaen, Morfa Nefyn, Pwllheli

The Dead Canary
♀ CARDIFF

Welcome to one of the Welsh capital's finest and friendliest bars in the heart of the city. The perfect spot for after-dinner drinks or to start a night out. And the cocktails are some of the best in these parts: unique (like the Pot Plant with rum, Chartreuse, kombucha and nettle), potent and totally tasty!

Barrack Ln, St Davids Centre, Cardiff

Belgrave Music Hall & Canteen
♀ LEEDS

A short stroll from Leeds train station and spread across three floors (including a roof terrace), the Belgrave Music Hall & Canteen is a go-to spot for live music, film and comedy. Beyond the entertainment there are good drinks and a vibe that'll keep you buzzing into the wee hours. An ideal place to hang out with pals.

Cross Belgrave St, Leeds

Hillhead Bookclub
♀ GLASGOW

Inside one of Glasgow's historic cinema buildings, near the Botanic Gardens, Hillhead Bookclub is one of the city's most eclectic venues to scoff a few cocktails or drams. It's a great spot to start your night with mates or dates. Attracting a bustling student crowd, it's got everything you need for an evening out. Just don't get too tipsy – you'll want to master your serve at 'Pingledon', their free ping-pong tables.

17 Vinicombe St, Glasgow

The Vaults
♀ LONDON

This unique spot is one of our favourite places to spend a night out – and part of the fun is finding it in the rabbit warren of disused railway arches underneath Waterloo station. The Vaults blends immersive theatre, live music and bars with buzzing tunes, cocktails and nibbles that are too good to miss. You'll find the unassuming entrance inside the Leake Street tunnel (a street art hotspot).

Leake St, London

Road Trippin'

Delightful drives that don't disappoint

↑ Penrhyn Quarry near Bethesda in North Wales

There's something special about getting out on the open road, the scenery whizzing by and your favourite tunes (or someone else's) sound-tracking the whole experience. We say it's not a proper road trip unless you've had at least one disagreement about the music!

Squabbles aside, our island nation is blessed with some of the finest routes in Europe. With an explorer's spirit and a zest for adventure, you can see so many epic places in a relatively short amount of time. From glacial valley passes and ford crossings to rugged coastal routes, you'll be spoilt for choice.

To help you get a footing, we've detailed some of our tyre-turning favourites, including long-weekend spins and mammoth Kerouac-style expeditions. For each trip we've recommended a suitable number of days to complete the drive, but this is just a guide – take as long or as little as you like. That said, even if you're steering by the seat of your pants rather than planning to perfection, it's a wise idea to make sure your car's in good health, bring essentials in case you break down or get lost, pack a road atlas (or download offline maps) and check the route for fuel stops or electric charging stations, snow flurries and roadworks before you set off.

Grown-up griping out of the way, it's time to put your seat belt on, adjust that rear-view mirror and put pedal to the metal. Oh, and somebody start the playlist! 🚗

North Coast 500

📍 **SCOTLAND**

Time to complete it:
Around seven to ten days,
depending on how many
stops you make.

—

Starting from:
Inverness (circular route)

—

Ending in:
Inverness (circular route)

Filled with glacial landscapes, unspoilt bays and rugged coastlines, the North Coast 500 takes you through the best of the Scottish Highlands. Totally windswept, idyllic and the kind of drive that'll leave you in awe, it's for those who love the unspoilt beauty of Scotland. There is a huge mix of historical sights and stunning vistas worth pulling over for, so be prepared to stop a fair bit on this 516-mile (830-kilometre) odyssey. You can start your trip at any point, in either direction, but we drove anti-clockwise, starting and ending in Inverness, which is well connected to the rest of Britain.

- Don't miss out on Dunnet Head, the most northerly point of the British mainland. Some travellers visit nearby John o'Groats (the most northern point between two inhabited spots in Great Britain – the southerly point being Land's End), but for sea views and puffins (in spring or early summer) RSPB Dunnet Head is the place to be.
- Driving down the west coast, stop off at the Seafood Shack in Ullapool for some of the freshest shellfish cooked to order. Open in the warmer summer months.
- See the waterfalls at Ugly Hollow (Corrieshalloch Gorge), one of the deepest gorges in Great Britain.
- To stretch your legs and blow the cobwebs out, take a stroll along the white sandy beach of Mellon Udrigle.
- Pull over at Rogie Falls (see p. 188 ☞) not far from Inverness to spot the leaping salmon in August and September. It's only a short walk from the main road.
- Keep a look out for Bealach na Bà Viewpoint on the twisting road that goes straight through Scotland's most dramatic glacial valley.

North East 250

♀ SCOTLAND

Time to complete it:
Around seven days
—

Starting from:
Ballindalloch, Aberdeen
Airport or Glenshee
(circular route)
—

Ending in:
Ballindalloch, Aberdeen
Airport or Glenshee
(circular route)

If you want to explore more of north-eastern Scotland and the Cairngorms, then the North East 250 is ideal. This circular adventure will take you through the unspoilt beauty of the Cairngorms National Park (**see p. 154** ☞) and Royal Deeside, with all its incredible castles, including the Queen's Scottish estate, Balmoral. Check the weather in advance if you're visiting in the colder months. The road between Tomintoul and Cock Bridge can get blocked by snow flurries.

- Soak up the north-eastern coast – think dramatic beaches, windswept landscapes – especially at Boddam, where you can check into the lighthouse keeper's cottages at Buchan Ness Lighthouse.
- Head into the historic fishing town of Portsoy and gorge at Portsoy Ice Cream, a family-run spot that's won plenty of awards for its tasty treats.
- Take in the views at Bow Fiddle Rock, an imposing sea arch.
- Stop for a dram of single malt Scotch at the Glenlivet Distillery. Oh, and buy a wee bottle for the driver to enjoy later. Sláinte!
- Stop by Crathes Castle and explore the history of this Scottish gem and its gardens.

North Wales Way
♀ WALES

Time to complete it:
A long weekend
—
Starting from:
Mold
—
Ending in:
Anglesey

Focusing on the most northerly parts of Wales, the North Wales Way follows a historic trading route and takes in some of Britain's prettiest coastal spots and coolest castles. Starting in Mold, close to the English border, you'll get to visit one of the country's smallest cities, St Asaph, before heading deeper into the northern heartland.

- See the iconic castles of Conwy, Caernarfon and Beaumaris (*see p. 32* ☞).
- Just off the main route, test your nerve on the huge ziplines at Penrhyn Quarry. Book online before you go and take some lozenges to soothe your throat after – you won't stop screaming!
- Enjoy a RibRide from Porth Daniel in Menai Bridge (ribride.co.uk). Board Velocity RIB, the world's fastest, for a speedy experience to remember! You'll be flying.
- End your trip on the island of Anglesey (*see p. 56* ☞) and see the most epic views from South Stack, over the Irish Sea (the perfect place for sunsets).

Lost in translation?
Yes, all the signs are bilingual, but it's great to understand some Welsh basics when driving. Look out for 'araf', which means slow (especially with all the winding roads) and 'gwasanaethau', meaning services (just in case you need the loo!).

Cambrian Way

♀ WALES

Not to be confused with the long-distance walking trail, this Cambrian Way road trip cuts through the middle of Wales from south to north (or vice versa), taking in some seriously dramatic inland spots along the way. Watch out for fighter jets that whoosh overhead and through the valleys. Sometimes they fly so low you can even make out the pilots!

....

Time to complete it:
Five to seven days

—

Starting from:
Cardiff

—

Ending in:
Llandudno

....

- Starting in Cardiff, head beyond Castell Coch (the fairytale castle) just outside the city.
- Drive deeper inland through the Brecon Beacons and the Elan Valley and swap the car for the narrow-gauge Brecon Mountain Railway that runs from Pant to Torpantau.
- Stop off at Machynlleth, the ancient capital of Wales (see p. 144 ☞).
- Make a pit stop in Dolgellau and grab a table at T. H. Roberts Coffee Shop, where you'll find some of the most delicious cakes in all the land. If you prefer savoury, go for the Welsh Rarebit – cheese on toast with leeks, beer and mustard.
- Test your surfing skills in the manmade lagoon at Adventure Parc Snowdonia.
- Play the arcades on Llandudno pier (Wales's longest) and stroll along the classic promenade.
- Look out for the Llandudno goats that live on the Great Orme, a whopping chunk of limestone that was named by the Vikings. The best way to reach the top is via the Great Orme Tramway.

Jurassic Route

♀ ENGLAND

Time to complete it:
Around four to five days

—

Starting from:
Exmouth

—

Ending in:
Old Harry Rocks

A firm favourite with us, this route won't include any T-rex encounters (thank goodness!), but you might come across the next best thing: Jurassic history and maybe even some dinosaur fossils. The Jurassic Coast, on England's south coast, includes 185 million years' worth of rocks, fossils and landforms, which are too incredible to miss.

- Start in Exmouth beyond A la Ronde, a quirky 16-sided house, and follow the A3052 through the centre of East Devon before stopping at Lyme Regis.
- Stop at Charmouth Beach for some fossil hunting – no tools are required, just patience and an eagle-eye. You're not allowed to dig into the cliffs, so visit in the winter months when the rough waves have done all the hard work for you.
- Strike a pose with the Cerne Abbas Giant. This 180-foot-tall (55-metre-tall) naked male figure is marked into the hillside with shallow trenches filled with chalk rubble.
- Cruise over to Corfe Castle (**see p. 134** ☞), stop off at Durdle Door (**see p. 97** ☞) and finish up at Old Harry Rocks.

Keep digging
Become a fossil-hunting aficionado with a private tour to get you up to speed. We booked a session with Jurassic Coast Guides (jurassiccoastguides.co.uk) to help us find and identify fossils along the beaches.

Coast to Coast Route

📍 ENGLAND

Time to complete it:
Around six to eight days
—
Starting from:
Kendal
—
Ending in:
Holy Island of Lindisfarne

Stretching right from the Irish to the North Sea, our 'Coast to Coast' route takes in northern England's most symbolic landscapes. You'll start in Kendal (where the mint cake comes from!) and head west toward the Lake District (**see p. 157** ☞), where you'll probably want to spend a few days exploring. Test your sailing skills on Windermere, hike up Scafell Pike (England's tallest mountain), visit Surprise View overlooking Derwentwater and try out paddleboarding on Ullswater (**see p. 176** ☞). Then it's time to get back on the road.

↑ Traipsing through the Lake District

- Stop in at Castlerigg near Keswick and marvel at the stone circle constructed during the Neolithic period – around 5000 years ago.
- Head further east towards the North Pennines. Park up at Garrigill and walk to Ashgill Force Waterfall. You can even stand behind the falls in certain conditions. Watch your step, though – the scramble down to the falls can get pretty slippery.
- Take a detour and try stargazing at Pow Hill Country Park – the lack of light pollution has earned it a Dark Sky Discovery Site designation. It's especially good if you're visiting during a meteor shower.
- North from the waterfall, stop off at the historic Roman ruins of Vindolanda or the Housesteads Roman Fort.
- Ramble along Hadrian's Wall (the Roman empire's most northerly frontier) to Sycamore Gap – a popular spot to snap the perfect pic of the wall (for more on Northumberland National Park, **see p. 161** ☞).
- Finally, head north-east (about a 2-hour drive) to the Northumberland Coast, where the sights of Bamburgh Castle (**see p. 27** ☞), Holy Island (**see p. 48** ☞) and the historic fishing villages of Craster and Seahouses will be waiting to greet you.

Iceni Route

♀ ENGLAND

Time to complete it:
Around five to seven days (including some time boating on the Broads)
—
Starting from:
Norwich
—
Ending in:
King's Lynn

Our Iceni Route takes in the pristine rural landscapes and historic settlements of Norfolk. The trip's named for the Iceni – a Brittonic tribe who lived in the region nearly 2000 years ago. They were a fiercely protective bunch, fighting off the invading Romans for decades. Starting in 'the fine city' of Norwich and ending near King's Lynn (or vice-versa), the trip takes in 200 miles (321 kilometres) of scenic countryside without a motorway in sight.

- First stop, Norwich Cathedral (see p. 70 ☞) and lunch at the city's famous market, which has been a permanent fixture here for 900 years!
- Head east to the Broads, a national park of waterways that spans Norfolk and neighbouring Suffolk and the largest protected wetland in the country. Swap your wheels for some paddles – rent a kayak at eight different locations from thecanoeman.com – or stay overnight on your own narrowboat. It's totally kitsch and so much fun.
- Up on the north coast, find sands that stretch for miles at Wells, with its colourful seaside huts, or Holkham Beach, part of the 18th-century Holkham Hall estate.
- Stop in at Sandringham, where you can explore the house and gardens and wander the woodland trails.
- To fill a hungry tummy, head over to Liquor & Loaded on Tower Street in King's Lynn. They create some messy mains like pulled pork waffle stacks that will leave even the hungriest of travellers stuffed.

⬆ Quiet cobbled streets in Norwich

↑ The Chipping Steps of Tetbury

Cotswolds Cottage Route

📍 **ENGLAND**

Time to complete it:
Around four to five days
—
Starting from:
Bath
—
Ending in:
Broadway

The Cotswolds takes the biscuit as one of our favourite spots in all of England, and we're not the only ones who think so – it is an AONB after all. Filled with the most picture-perfect cottages and idyllic villages, it's a delightful contrast for city-dwellers like us. The route begins in the Roman city of Bath (**see p. 77** ☞) and then heads north to Castle Combe about 30 minutes' drive away. This 700-year-old village (built in part using stones from the castle that lends it its name) is a treasure trove of higgledy-piggledy cottages, a taste of what's to come …

- After Castle Combe, the drive takes you up the 'spine of the Cotswolds' towards Tetbury, a quaint market town. Visit the gardens at Highgrove House while you're here – it's Prince Charles's family residence.
- Head towards bustling Cirencester for quirky shops and churches, and check out the Roman artefacts at the Corinium Museum.
- Fifteen minutes east of Cirencester is Bibury, home of the Cotswolds' most-photographed street – Arlington Row. Visit first thing in the morning or last thing in the afternoon if you want to miss the majority of the summer crowds. It can get busy.
- Other vivacious villages worth pulling over for include Burford, Bourton-on-the-Water, the Slaughters and Stow-on-the-Wold, before finishing in Broadway. Each have their own unique charm, plenty of tearooms for scones and clotted cream, and even an adorable model village (in Bourton-on-the-Water).

The Literary Way

📍 ENGLAND

Time to complete it:
Around four to five days
—

Starting from:
Norwich
—

Ending in:
Oxford

Our bookworm route takes in some of England's most esteemed centres of literature, learning and literary greats, so bring a good book to accompany your travels. It all kicks off in England's first UNESCO City of Literature, Norwich (see p. 70 ☞), which houses the National Centre for Writing and some lovely little book shops (we're looking at you, Book Hive). Hit the open road and head for the cathedral city of Ely. This small centre is steeped in history, especially with its imposing cathedral (which stood in for Westminster Abbey in TV show *The Crown*) and Oliver Cromwell's house. Then it's on to Cambridge, Warwick, Stratford-upon-Avon and Oxford – you're in for an epic adventure!

↑ Being a-maze-d at Blenheim Palace

Top tip
If you prefer, you can easily end the Literary Way in London and explore the Charles Dickens Museum in Holborn or Keats House in Hampstead to learn more about the poet's life and writing.

↑ Lord Leycester Hospital in Warwick (not a real hospital)

- In Cambridge (**see p. 184** ☞), try your hand at punting on the River Ely, explore King's College Chapel and see the city from above at Great St Mary's church tower.
- Make your way west to Warwick, about 1 hour and 40 minutes, and visit medieval marvels – the 14th-century Lord Leycester Hospital and Warwick Castle.
- Not far from here is Stratford-upon-Avon, William Shakespeare's home! Visit the playwright's birthplace on Henley Street, explore Hall's Croft (the Jacobean home of Shakespeare's daughter) and Anne Hathaway's Cottage (the family home of Shakespeare's wife).
- Catch a performance at the Royal Shakespeare Theatre. Book in advance – tickets sell out fast in the popular summer months.
- Make a beeline for Blenheim Palace (**see p. 147** ☞), where Winston Churchill once lived. Check the website for the annual literary festival. Don't forget to pop into the cosy Woodstock Bookshop (woodstockbookshop.co.uk) – they stock new, second-hand and out-of-print books.
- Arrive in Oxford (**see p. 87** ☞), home for a time to university English faculty and friends C. S. Lewis and J. R. R. Tolkien. There's lots to see, including Oxford Castle, Oxford University's Museum of Natural History and the Radcliffe Camera reading rooms.

The Big One

📍 **ENGLAND AND SCOTLAND**

Time to complete it:
Around three to four weeks
—
Starting from:
Land's End
—
Ending in:
John o'Groats

Stretching from the Penwith Heritage Coast in Cornwall, all the way to Caithness in northern Scotland, this is one chunky trip that takes in the best of England and Scotland. Sorry, Wales, you're gorgeous, but there was only so much gas in the tank! At well over 1300 miles (2090 kilometres), this is the kind of adventure that's as much about the drive as it is about the destinations. It incorporates bits of some of the other road trips as well as plenty of parks, trails, natural sites, cities and historical hotspots we recommend throughout the book.

↑ Vintage wheels in Broadway, Cotswolds

- Start at the most westerly point of England – Land's End – and wind your way up the coast to St Ives.
- Travelling east through Cornwall, stop in Bodmin (and watch out for that infamous beast – a wildcat rumoured to stalk the moorland) and then drive on to Plymouth. Along the way, stop off at the Rod & Line Inn (in Tideford) for a proper pub lunch made from locally grown produce. It's also great for a roast dinner if you're visiting on a Sunday.
- Stay a while in Salcombe on the South Devon coast and gorge yourself silly on freshly cooked crab at The Crab Shed. Their crab linguine is everything. Ask for extra chilli for a kick!
- Head to Salisbury, taking in some of the Jurassic Route (**see p. 202** ☞) from Exmouth. We recommend touring the cathedral and eyeing up Magna Carta (**see p. 131** ☞).
- Wend your way north-eastwards to Wells (**see p. 68** ☞) before hopping on over to Cheddar Gorge (**see p. 98** ☞) for glorious hikes and tasty cheese.
- Break your trip in Bath (**see p. 77** ☞) for Roman relics, Georgian splendour and a geothermal spa with views of the city.
- Cruise through the Cotswolds, following the route on **page 205,** and then launch into the bookish delights of the Literary Way via Warwick and Stratford-upon-Avon (**see p. 206** ☞).
- Leaving Shakespeare's birthplace behind, drive 2 hours to Buxton in Derbyshire – peruse the Pavilion Gardens and the grand Buxton Crescent – and use it as a base to explore the Peak District (**see p. 150** ☞).
- Further north, join the Coast to Coast route (**see p. 203** ☞) at Kendal and make your way to Northumberland and the otherworldly Holy Island (**see p. 48** ☞).
- Storm into Scotland via Berwick-upon-Tweed, following the east coast to explore the bright lights of Edinburgh (**see p. 65** ☞). Then, leave the city in your rear-view and set your sights on Loch Lomond (**see p. 160** ☞).
- Head beyond Glencoe and Fort William and say hello to the Highlands for dramatic scenery and captivating castles. Once you reach the west coast, you're on track for the North Coast 500 (**see p. 198** ☞) – taking in Poolewe, the Corrieshalloch Gorge (with its amazing Falls of Measach), Ullapool and Kylesku.
- Revel in the rugged coastline around Cape Wrath and drive through Tongue towards Dunnet Head (the most northerly point in Great Britain), before toasting your success over tea at the Stacks Coffee House & Bistro at John o'Groats.

Travel Tips from the Brits

If you're travelling to our shores for the very first time, first off, a massive welcome – we hope you have the most amazing adventure in Great Britain.

Over the years, we've collected heaps of practical tips to make our trips that bit easier, cheaper and more fun! From getting around and currency queries to bagging the biggest discounts, we've jotted down some essentials you need to know when visiting for the first time. And, as always, we're just a message away if you need any more tips!

Trains

With loads of lines and services crisscrossing our gorgeous island, travelling by train is a (usually) reliable, safe, and great way to explore. One thing to note is pricing. It can be a little expensive compared to some other countries, but there are ways to keep costs down. Firstly, be sure to avoid peak times when prices go up substantially. These are typically Monday to Friday 06:30–09:30 and 15:30–18:30. Even if you depart one minute outside of these hours, you can buy an off-peak fare and save a lot of money.

To get some of the lowest prices, book as far in advance as possible. Typically, advanced tickets are significantly cheaper and can be bought from the train service's website. Though, unlike some other train tickets, you will need to travel on the specified service, so you can't rock up late and catch the next train.

Also, don't forget about railcards! These can offer at least a third off the cost of train travel. Some are network-specific, and some apply no matter where you travel. The price varies depending on card type, but you can usually make your money back after two longer train trips. Check out railcard.co.uk to see which best suits your circumstances and eligibility. If you're unsure, ask at a train station ticket office.

Money

Visa, Mastercard and contactless phone payments are widely taken across Great Britain and can be used for most transactions in shops and restaurants. That being said, if you are visiting a farmers' market or local stalls, you might need cash. American Express is also accepted here, but to a lesser extent than Visa and Mastercard. For this reason, always carry a back-up card.

Holidays and opening hours

Lots of places are open seven days a week but with reduced hours on a Sunday. This typically applies to shops, banks and currency exchange, but most restaurants are open normal hours on a Sunday.

While travelling around Great Britain, you might hear the words 'bank holiday'. These are set dates throughout the year when lots of people will have time off. Typically, banks and services will be closed but shops, most attractions and restaurants will still be open, albeit at reduced hours. Bank holidays differ between England, Wales and Scotland – check out gov.uk/bank-holidays for more information. Also, don't forget that nearly everywhere (apart from a select few pubs and restaurants) will be closed on Christmas Day.

Museums and galleries

All of the UK's 'national museums' are free to enter (although you might have to pay an entry fee for special exhibitions), as are a number of other museums and galleries up and down the country. Take London, for example. There you can visit the Tate Modern, the British Museum, the National Portrait Gallery and many others without spending a penny! Though, a donation is always welcome.

Attraction discounts

Don't just buy your tickets at the venue for bigger attractions. You can usually secure a discount if you book in advance. Attractions often have ticket discounts if you buy directly from their website, so always check this out first. Oh, and if you're travelling by train, head to daysoutguide.co.uk where your train tickets can secure you two-for-one deals and more.

Check to see if your trip coincides with a specific holiday or event. For instance, on St Andrew's Day (30 November) in Scotland, lots of attractions are free to enter. This means you can visit Edinburgh Castle and countless other spots without reaching into your pocket. Head to ticketgiveaway.co.uk to find out more. Also, if you're exploring England, find out if you're visiting on any Heritage Open Days. These are specific days (usually in September) when lots of properties, including those closed to the public, are open to wander around. See full details at heritageopendays.org.uk.

Also, don't forget that most attractions, including historic National Trust properties, will also offer discounts for children, seniors, families and large groups, as well as for certain visitors with eligible IDs, including students, disabled visitors and their carers, and the military. Discounts vary, but it's always worth checking.

Driving

One thing to remember: we drive on the left! Also, lots of (though, not all) cars will be manual or 'stick'. If you're not comfortable driving a manual car, make sure to specify 'automatic' to your rental company when booking. Once you're out and about, you'll find our roads can be very narrow, especially in the countryside. If you want to avoid these, motorways and 'A' roads will be the wider (but busier) routes to take.

Also, it's worth remembering that driving times between cities can be longer (or shorter) than taking the train, depending on how well connected they are by road or rail links. For instance, it's typically quicker to take the train from London to Edinburgh than driving. Check an online map tool – Google Maps works very well in Great Britain – to see the respective journey times. Sometimes it's easier to hire cars in multiple cities you plan on visiting (than driving longer distances in just one hire car).

Plugs and voltage

We have a G-type plug socket here. You'll need plugs with three rectangular pins in a triangular pattern or a converter to get your all-important items charging. We have a 230V supply voltage and 50Hz.

Airport transfers

Most airports will have a public transport option, private car rentals and taxi ranks to arrange transfers once you arrive. If you fly into Heathrow, you can catch the Tube from the terminal. This will take you into central London and beyond. Alternatively, you can hop in a black cab – though these are usually more expensive than booking an Uber. Luton, Stansted, Gatwick and Manchester airports all have frequent train services, which you don't need to book in advance. For Edinburgh, you can also hop on the tram or bus, and for smaller airports like Cardiff, you'll need to take a taxi or the bus.

Train station transfers

Most major train stations are in the heart of larger towns and cities. Some cities have more than one train station, which are well connected by public buses, trams or subway trains. Most will also have a taxi rank, making it really easy to hop in a car if you don't fancy lugging your bags across town. The same goes for St Pancras International (where the Eurostar arrives).

The countryside

While exploring the great outdoors, you should stick to the principles of the Countryside Code. It covers how to respect the environment you're exploring, the rights you have on specific footpaths and the differences between National Trails (nationaltrail.co.uk) and 'open access' areas where you can explore without having to stay on the paths. Read the code here: gov.uk/government/publications/the-countryside-code.

Index

All images © Yaya Onalaja-Aliu and Lloyd Griffiths except the following: pages 24 (bottom), 31, 32, 33, 34, 43, 44, 45, 46, 47, 50, 51, 52, 53, 56, 57, 66, 67, 72, 73, 74, 75, 90, 91, 99, 100, 103, 113, 118, 120 (top), 121, 123, 141, 144, 145, 160, 161, 178, 190, 191, 192, 201 all courtesy iStock Photos.

Published in 2021 by Hardie Grant Travel,
a division of Hardie Grant Publishing

Hardie Grant Travel (Melbourne)
Wurundjeri Country
Building 1, 658 Church Street
Richmond, Victoria 3121

Hardie Grant Travel (Sydney)
Gadigal Country
Level 7, 45 Jones Street
Ultimo, NSW 2007

www.hardiegrant.com/au/travel

Hand Luggage Only: Great Britain
ISBN 9781741177589

10 9 8 7 6 5 4 3 2 1

Publisher Melissa Kayser
Project editor Megan Cuthbert
Editor Sarah Herman
Editorial assistance Rosanna Dutson
Proofreader Lucy York
Cartographer Emily Maffei
Design Murray Batten
Typesetting Hannah Schubert
Index Max McMaster

Maps in this publication were made with Natural Earth
@ naturalearthdata.com

A catalogue record for this book is available from the National Library of Australia

Hardie Grant acknowledges the Traditional Owners of the Country on which we work, the Wurundjeri people of the Kulin Nation and the Gadigal people of the Eora Nation, and recognises their continuing connection to the land, waters and culture. We pay our respects to their Elders past, present and emerging.

Colour reproduction by Hannah Schubert and Splitting Image Colour Studio

Printed and bound in China by LEO Paper Products LTD.